WITHDRAWN
UTSA LIBRARIES

**Bargaining:
Monopoly Power
versus Union Power**

A Publication of
the Joint Center for Urban Studies
of the Massachusetts Institute
of Technology
and Harvard University

The MIT Press
Cambridge, Massachusetts,
and London, England

**Bargaining:
Monopoly Power
versus Union Power**

George de Menil

Copyright © 1971 by
The Massachusetts Institute of Technology

This book was designed by The MIT Press Design Department.
It was set in Monotype Baskerville
by Wolf Composition Company
printed and bound
by Vail-Ballou Press, Inc.
in the United States of America.

All rights reserved. No part of this book may be reproduced in any form or by any means, electronic or mechanical, including photocopying, recording, or by any information storage and retrieval system, without permission in writing from the publisher.

ISBN 0 262 04035 2 (hardcover)

Library of Congress catalog card number: 70-158646

To Lois

Contents

Preface	xi

1 Introduction   1

2 Bargaining Theories—A Survey   4
2.1. Introduction   4
2.2. Game Theory and the Bargaining Problem   4
2.3. The Nash Theory of Bargaining   8
2.4. Alternative Bargaining Theories   14
2.5. Summary   20

3 A Nash Model of Bilateral Monopoly   21
3.1. Introduction   21
3.2. Assumptions   21
3.3. A Model of the Firm   23
3.4. Summary   27

4 Comparative Statics of the Nash Model   29
4.1. Introduction   29

4.2. Bilateral Monopoly and Monopoly Contrasted	29
4.3. Forward Shifting of a Profits Tax	31
4.4. Backward Shifting of a Profits Tax	32
4.5. Money Wages and the General Price Level	36
4.6. Summary	39

5
A Testable Wage Equation 40

5.1. Introduction	40
5.2. An Equilibrium Wage Equation	40
5.3. Specification of Variables	43
5.4. Dynamics of Adjustment	46

6
Wage Rates, Productivity, and Variable Construction 51

6.1. Introduction	51
6.2. Wage Rates and Average Hourly Earnings	52
6.3. Construction of Overtime Series for Missing Years	55
6.4. Importance of Compositional and Seasonal Effects	59

6.5. Estimation of Long-Run Value Productivity	62
6.6. Nonunion Wages and Turnover Rates	70
6.7. Summary	73

7
Estimation Results — 75
7.1. Introduction	75
7.2. Industry Phillips Curves	75
7.3. Bargaining Equations	77
7.4. Qualifications	84
7.5. Summary	85

8
Conclusion — 86

Data Appendix — 90
Table A–1. Overtime Hours	90
Table A–2. Average Hourly Earnings Excluding Overtime	91
Table A–3. Gross Output per Man Hour at Full Capacity	91
Table A–4. Value Productivity at Full Capacity	92
Table A–5. Seasonally Adjusted Quarterly Layoff Rates	92

Table A–6.
Seasonal Factors for Layoff Rates   92
Table A–7.
The Nonunion Wage and the Cost of Living   93

Bibliography   109

**Publications of the Joint Center for
Urban Studies**   116

Index   119

Preface

This book is an outgrowth of a Ph.D. thesis on wage movements which I wrote at M.I.T. in 1967. The basic work on this subject is an article by Phillips (1958) which describes the trade-off, now known as the Phillips curve, between the rate of change of wages and unemployment. When I began my thesis, Phillips' article had already seen many extensions and modifications, some of them the work of George Perry, who had also written an M.I.T. thesis on the subject in 1961, and whose book, *Unemployment, Money Wage Rates, and Inflation* (1966), had just appeared. There was, however, an important aspect of the problem which I felt had not yet been adequately treated, namely the influence of collective bargaining on wage movements. The standard approach to this problem involved accounting for the special characteristics of unionized industries simply by adding one or more additional variables to Phillips' original equation. The prime contender, and the one which was employed by Perry and by Eckstein and Wilson (1962) for instance, was the profit rate. However, I felt that the arguments adduced for relating wages to profits—which depended on concepts as difficult to define as "ability to pay," "the cost of a strike," and "equity"—were unsatisfactory, and that a formal model of bargaining was needed to give substance to these concepts. The task I set for myself in the thesis was to construct and test such a model.

When, two years after the completion of the thesis, I began writing a book on the subject, I decided to change the basic model radically and to update the empirical work and re-estimate the equations. The result is the present volume, a new and much shorter work than the thesis. The only part of the book that has not been completely rewritten is the account, now in Chapter 6, of the extensive job of data construction which had to be undertaken before any tests could be made. Since many of these data have been constructed or refined by me and have not previously been published, an appendix of data tables has been added.

My greatest thanks go to Edwin Kuh, both as my teacher in econometrics and as the supervisor of my thesis. His generous and untiring encouragement and advice were immensely valuable. I am also deeply appreciative of Robert Solow's careful guidance and insights as a second reader of the thesis, and of the criticisms and ideas of Anthony Atkinson, Robert Bishop and Michael Piore. Ira J. Miller and Allen P. Keesee provided excellent research assistance. Inez Crandall, Manya Vas, and Betty Kaminski cheerfully typed successive versions of the manuscript. I am grateful for the support of the Joint Center for Urban Studies of Harvard University and M.I.T., where I was a student associate during the year 1965–66.

Finally, I thank my wife, Lois de Menil, for her unlimited patience and lucid advice. My gratitude is greater than can be expressed in a phrase in a preface.

George de Menil

Princeton, N.J.
February 1971

**Bargaining:
Monopoly Power
versus Union Power**

Introduction

Markets in which the standard models of competition, monopoly, and monopolistic competition do not apply are among the most difficult subjects for economic analysis. The labor market in highly unionized and highly concentrated industries is a case in point. This study deals with wage determination in such labor markets.

The literature on the subject divides into untested, abstract bargaining models on the one hand and empirical studies relating wages to "bargaining variables" without the benefit of formal theory on the other. The present work attempts to bridge the gap. A wage equation is derived formally from a bargaining model and then tested on data for manufacturing industries in the United States.

This involves first finding a good bargaining theory. Thus, Chapter 2 starts with a discussion of bargaining theories. The theory of bargaining in Nash [1950, 1953] is chosen as being the most applicable. The next step is to build a model of the firm under bilateral monopoly—the situation in which one employer faces one union—based on Nash's bargaining theory. This is done in Chapter 3. Assumptions are made concerning the product-demand curve, production function, capital supply, supply of union members, and the utility functions of the employer and the union. These assumptions, plus two hypotheses from Nash's theory, determine the wage rate, employment, capital stock, output, price, and profits under bilateral monopoly. The comparative statics of the model are then examined in Chapter 4.

Since the principal objective of this study is the derivation and testing of a wage equation, it is the wage equation in the model of Chapters 3 and 4 which is of greatest interest. In Chapter 5 this equation is changed into a form in which it can be estimated.

The remainder of the book deals with empirical testing of the wage equation. Variable construction is discussed in Chapter 6, and the results of estimation and tests are reported in Chapter 7. The population used to test the equation consists of highly unionized two-digit manufacturing industries in the United States for which data were available. The ideal data for testing it would have been those on individual contracts between an employer and a union. However, when this study began, such data did not exist,[1] and constructing them would have involved considerable difficulty. Given the absence of individual contract data, the finest category for which data on all the necessary variables were available were two-digit industries in the manufacturing sector. The fact that they are used in many other studies[2] is evidence of the lack of a good alternative. The desire for comparability provides another good reason for using the two-digit industry data.

In Chapter 7 estimates of the wage equation are compared with Phillips curves estimated for the same industries. The form of this wage equation is such that it can be viewed as a Phillips curve to which some "bargaining variables" have been added. The conclusion reached in Chapter 7 is that this wage equation explains the quarterly movement of average hourly earnings in the test industries better than the Phillips curve. In other words, the additional bargaining variables significantly reduce unexplained variance. This statistical result in itself is not new. Other studies[3] have already shown that fits are improved by the addition of bargaining variables to the

1. Hamermesh [1970] is a recent study using individual contract data collected for the study.
2. See Eckstein and Wilson [1962], McGuire and Rapping [September-October, 1968], Pierson [1968], Throop [1968], and Wachter [1970].
3. See Eckstein and Wilson [1962], Kuh [1967], and Perry [1966].

Phillips curve. What is new is that the nature and form of these bargaining variables were carefully derived from a formal theory of bargaining.

2

Bargaining Theories — A Survey

2.1.
Introduction

The two-person bargaining problem is the determination of the quantities of goods that will be exchanged between isolated individuals. The orthodox position concerning it was for a long time that, if a stalemate is to be avoided, the two parties will settle in a range on their contract curve in which they both benefit from trade but that the precise point on which they will settle is indeterminate.[1] This position was challenged in the early 1930s, and since then a series of bargaining theories have been proposed which offer determinate solutions. In fact, today there are so many bargaining theories with determinate solutions that the principal difficulty is deciding which one to choose.

However one of them does stand out in the literature as more widely accepted than the others. This is Nash's theory.[2] The purpose of this chapter is to describe this theory and to explain its choice as our point of departure.

2.2.
Game Theory and the Bargaining Problem

Nash's theory is a branch of the theory of games of von Neumann and Morgenstern [1953]. One of the basic postulates of game theory is that each individual has a utility function that is unique up to an order preserving linear transformation.[3] Another frequently used assumption is that each individual has full knowledge of the rules

---

1. An excellent summary of contributions to the literature on the bargaining problem during the nineteenth and early twentieth centuries appears in Machlup and Taber [1960].
2. Nash [1950, 1953].
3. These have come to be known as the von Neumann–Morgenstern utilities.

5 Game Theory and the Bargaining Problem

of the game, of the objective payoffs associated with every possible outcome, and of the utility functions of his opponents.

In game-theoretic terms, the bargaining problem is a special case of the general class of cooperative, non-zero-sum games. It is non-zero-sum because there are gains from trade. An increase in one party's utility does not necessarily result in a decline in any opponent's utility. It is cooperative because the parties are free to reach explicit agreements. It is often assumed that the rules of negotiation are such that no party has a strategic advantage over another.

> Schelling criticizes this last assumption that the move structure of the game is symmetric. He claims that it transforms the bargaining game into one that is like a race between two men, each knowing that the other is just as good a racer as he. The winner gets the prize, but in the case of a tie the prize is split between the two runners. If it is determined in advance that the outcome will always be a tie, Schelling asks, why should the men race? The answer of the theorist of symmetric games is that he is not interested in whether the men race or not. His interest is in the outcome, in the fact that the prize will be divided evenly between the two men. See Schelling [1960], Appendix B, particularly pp. 275, 276.

Bargaining games may involve n persons, but since negotiations between an employer and a union involve only two, discussion will be limited here to two-person bargaining games.

The concept of threat plays an important role in game theory. A threat is a conditional commitment to a definite course of action. It is conditional on the demand associated with the threat not being met. The important point is that threats must be carried out. Non-zero-sum games are fixed-threat games if there is only one possible state of conflict, and variable-threat games if there are several possible states of conflict associated with the choice of different threats by the two parties.

Bargaining between an employer and a union will be treated here as a fixed-threat game. This amounts to assuming that the only damage each party can do to the other is to refuse to trade.

There are threats other than strikes. The union may threaten a slowdown, or violence. The analysis here will abstract from these possibilities. Strictly speaking, even under that assumption, collective bargaining is a variable-threat game, but a very special variable-threat game to which the theory of fixed-threat games is immediately applicable. Even if the only thing a union can do to an employer is to strike, strikes are of varying duration. However, it turns out that it will always be in the interest of one of the two parties to threaten an indefinite strike. A thorough explanation of this point would require discussion of the theory of variable-threat bargaining. (See Nash [1953] or, for a less technical account, Bishop [1963].)

Let s be the duration of the threatened strike, which we shall call the "threat instrument." Let the ratio of the cost of a conflict to party 1 over the cost of a conflict to party 2 be some function $f(s)$. If there were two instruments, say x_1 and x_2, then the relative cost of a conflict would be $f(x_1, x_2)$, and that function might have a saddle point, at which each party would have minimized the greatest value of the ratio of cost of conflict to him over cost of conflict to his opponent that his opponent could inflict on him. One could argue that that point would determine the actual choice of threats in a variable-threat game. But in our case, with relative strike costs dependent on only one variable, there cannot be a saddle point. Since the party who threatens the longest strike is the one whose threat is most effective, one of the two parties will always threaten indefinite strike. Though there is a range of threats to choose from, only one is ever chosen—the threat of withdrawal from the industry.

The notion that the only fundamentally relevant threat is the threat of withdrawal from the industry has important implications for applying any static, game-theoretic model of the bargaining problem to labor negotiations. It means that the outcome of negotiations will depend not on the cost of a limited strike (as many economists have argued) but on the cost of withdrawal from the industry. The cost of a limited strike can influence the outcome only if it acts as a proxy for the cost of withdrawal from the industry. The Hicksian bargaining theories discussed later in this chapter seem to imply a somewhat different view of the duration of the no-trade threat than the one just presented. However, the relation of these theories to von Neumann–Morgenstern game theory is unclear. And since game theory offers the best and most solid foundation available, our interpretation of threats is the one outlined above.

7 Game Theory and the Bargaining Problem

Game-theoretic analysis of the fixed-threat bargaining problem focuses on the utility frontier and the threat point. The utility frontier is the mapping onto the utility space of the permissible range of the contract curve.

This mapping will not always be concave to the origin. If it is not, but if probability agreements are feasible ("I win half the time, you win the rest of the time"), the portions of the frontier which are convex to the origin can be bridged by straight lines. The corrected utility frontier will be either a straight line or concave to the origin.

The coordinates of the threat point are the utilities of the two parties when the fixed threats are realized. In what follows reference will sometimes be made to the "utility increments frontier." This is the frontier of increments in utility from the threat point. When the threat point is placed at the origin, the utility frontier is also the utility increments frontier.

The game theorist's approach to finding the solution to any conflict situation is to state certain conditions which he believes any agreement between rational parties must satisfy, and then to consider whether these conditions determine a unique outcome, a set of possible outcomes, or whether they are inconsistent.

According to one interpretation, the solution of the game theorist is a positive description of the agreement that any pair of rational players will reach;[4] according to another, it is a description of the agreement that a "fair" arbitrator will suggest.[5] In the latter case, the statement of the required characteristics of the outcome may be viewed as a statement of the principles of the arbitrator. If the latter's principles are so clear and compelling that the two parties

---

4. For a strong statement of the view that the Nash solution is a positive description of the behavior of rational bargainers, see Harsanyi [October 1962] and the exchange of views between Wagner [1957, 1958] and Harsanyi [April 1958], and Bishop [1963].

5. This is the view of Luce and Raiffa [1957], pp. 121–124.

always reach, of their own accord, just the agreement he would have suggested, then the two interpretations agree.

One of the characteristics that all game theorists ascribe to the outcome of a game with rational players is that the strategies of the two players which result in this outcome are equilibrium strategies. This means that if player 1 knew ahead of time what the strategy of player 2 was going to be he would have no incentive to change his own strategy. Each strategy is the best possible one to play against the other.

In a zero-sum game with mixed strategies (that is, where probability mixtures of determinate strategies are permitted), this condition uniquely determines the value of the game. The minimax theorem states that there is always at least one pair of equilibrium mixed strategies, and that if there is more than one, they all bring equal utilities to the two players. In a cooperative, non-zero-sum game, there is an infinity of equilibrium pairs of strategies, including any point on the contract curve. Additional requirements must be formulated if a unique point is to be selected as the solution.

2.3.

The Nash Theory of Bargaining

The game theorist analyzing a two-person, fixed-threat bargaining game typically may look for principles that have the power of "coordinating the expectations" of the two players.[6] If "I know that the outcome must be X and you know it, and I know that you know it, and so on," then the outcome will be X.

Nash argued that there were four of these principles and that they were the following:

A1. *Efficiency:* The solution must lie on the utility frontier.

[6]. The phrase is that of Schelling.

A2. *Symmetry:* If the utility increments frontier is symmetrical, the solution gives equal utility increments to both parties.

A3. *Transformation invariance:* The solution is not altered by a linear, order-preserving transformation of the utility function of either party.

A4. *Independence of irrelevant alternatives:* Suppose the solution for a given utility frontier has been found. If that utility frontier is unfavorably altered anywhere except at the solution point, the solution is not changed.[7]

The efficiency axiom has always been a part of accepted economic analysis of the bargaining problem and needs no further comment. The symmetry axiom has powerful intuitive appeal. If the utilities of the two parties were comparable and the utility frontier were symmetric, it would be natural for both parties to expect to share equal amounts of utility increase as they moved from the threat point to an agreement. The Nash solution can be viewed as an extension of this basic notion, permitting it to be applied to situations where the utilities of the two parties are not comparable.[8]

The transformation-invariance axiom expresses operationally the impossibility of comparing the utilities of the two parties. If broadly accepted equity considerations would influence the outcome of union–employer bargaining, bargaining would depend on interpersonal utility comparisons. However, it shall be assumed in this study that the outcome of collective bargaining negotiations is primarily a function of objective factors and not of equity con-

7. The discussion of Nash's axioms that follows borrows heavily from Bishop [1963].
8. Harsanyi's slightly different view is that "Nash's theory of bargaining (with given threats) is fundamentally a generalization of (the symmetry principle) for the more general case of asymmetric situations." See Harsanyi [April 1956], p. 147.

siderations.[9] The transformation-invariance axiom is the expression of this assumption.

The axiom of the independence of irrelevant alternatives is best explained by means of an example. Consider the game whose utility increments frontier has been drawn in Figure 2.1a. The threat point has been placed at the origin. The maximum utility increment each party can obtain is set at 100. Suppose the two parties have reached an agreement placing them at the point N. Independence of irrelevant alternatives means that any change in the game that restricts the outcomes but leaves the threat point and the original solution point in the game does not alter the solution. If the game of Fig. 2.1a is changed to 2.1b or 2.1c, the solution still remains at N. Another example involves government intervention in the activities of two bilateral monopolists. If the intervention leaves them free to reach the same agreement they would have reached before the intervention, and if it leaves no-trade positions unchanged, then it has no effect.[10]

What Nash proved is that these four axioms—efficiency, symmetry, transformation invariance, and independence of irrelevant alternatives—determine one (and, if the utility frontier is quasi-concave, only one) solution point. This is the point where the product of utility increments from the threat point is a maximum.

The characteristics of this solution are best described by means of an example. Suppose two parties are negotiating an agreement whereby the first party will receive a quantity to be determined of a good π and the second party a quantity to be determined of a

---

9. The influence of public opinion on major contracts may make this a weak assumption for some industries.
10. This example is due to Bishop [1963], p. 581. Bishop considers it evidence of the weakness of the axiom.

The Nash Theory of Bargaining

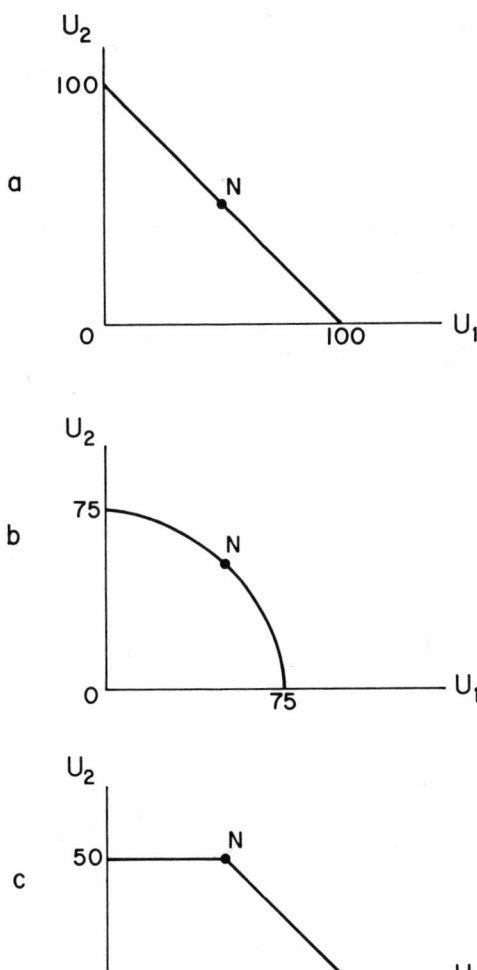

Figure 2.1. The Nash Point Is Independent of Irrelevant Alternatives

good B. On the contract curve, let $\pi = \pi(B)$; $d\pi/dB < 0$. Assume that if the two parties do not reach an agreement they will receive π^0 and B^0. Let the utility which each derives from its benefits be $U^e(\pi)$ and $U^u(B)$. Then the coordinates of the threat point are $U^e(\pi^0)$ and $U^u(B^0)$, and the utility increments from the threat point to any agreement are $U^e(\pi) - U^e(\pi^0)$ and $U^u(B) - U^u(B^0)$. The product of these increments is a maximum, where

$$\frac{\dfrac{(\partial U^e/\partial \pi)(\partial \pi/\partial B)}{U^e(\pi) - U^e(\pi^0)}}{\dfrac{\partial U^u/\partial B}{U^u(B) - U^u(B^0)}} = -1, \tag{2.1}$$

which can also be recognized as the point where the elasticity of the utility increments frontier is minus one.

The first-order condition for a maximum of Prod = $[U^e(\pi) - U^e(\pi^0)] \times [U^u(B) - U^u(B^0)]$ is

$$\frac{d[\text{Prod}]}{dB} = \frac{\partial U^e}{\partial \pi}\frac{\partial \pi}{\partial B}U^u(B) + U^e(\pi)\frac{\partial U^u}{\partial B} - U^e(\pi^0)\frac{\partial U^u}{\partial B} - U^u(B^0)\frac{\partial U^e}{\partial \pi}\frac{\partial \pi}{\partial B} = 0,$$

or

$$[U^u(B) - U^u(B^0)]\frac{\partial U^e}{\partial \pi}\frac{\partial \pi}{\partial B} = -[U^e(\pi) - U^e(\pi^0)]\frac{\partial U^u}{\partial B}.$$

By rearranging terms one obtains Eq. 2.1.

The utility increments frontier is the function relating $U^e(\pi) - U^e(\pi^0)$ to $U^u(B) - U^u(B^0)$. Its slope is

$$\frac{(\partial U^e/\partial \pi)(\partial \pi/\partial B)}{\partial U^u/\partial B}.$$

Its elasticity is thus the left-hand side of Eq. 2.1.

This maximum is unique—and therefore the Nash solution is unique—if and only if $(d^2[\text{Prod}]/dB^2) < 0$ for all values of B. Differentiation shows that

$$\frac{d^2[\text{Prod}]}{dB^2} = [U^u(B) - U^u(B^0)]\left[\left(\frac{\partial \pi}{\partial B}\right)^2 \frac{\partial^2 U^e}{\partial \pi^2} + \frac{\partial U^e}{\partial \pi}\frac{\partial^2 \pi}{\partial B^2}\right]$$
$$+ 2\frac{\partial U^e}{\partial \pi}\frac{\partial \pi}{\partial B}\frac{\partial U^u}{\partial B}$$
$$+ [U^e(\pi) - U^e(\pi^0)]\frac{\partial^2 U^u}{\partial B^2}.$$

A sufficient condition for this to be less than zero is that none of the following quantities be greater than zero:
$$\frac{\partial^2 U^e}{\partial \pi^2}, \quad \frac{\partial^2 \pi}{\partial B^2}, \quad \frac{\partial^2 U^u}{\partial B^2}.$$
In a case which will come to be of particular interest later,
$$\frac{\partial^2 U^e}{\partial \pi^2} = \frac{\partial^2 \pi}{\partial B^2} = \frac{\partial^2 U^u}{\partial B^2} = 0.$$
Here the second-order condition
$$\frac{d^2[\text{Prod}]}{dB^2} = \frac{\partial U^e}{\partial \pi} \frac{\partial \pi}{\partial B} \frac{\partial U^u}{\partial B} < 0$$
is satisfied for all values of B.

To simplify still further, suppose that what the two parties are bargaining over is a fixed quantity of a homogeneous good, such as money. Then $\pi + B =$ constant. Let each of them receive nothing if they end in a stalemate. Without loss of generality the two utility functions can be rescaled so that $U^e(0) = U^u(0) = 0$. In this case, Eq. 2.1 becomes[11]

$$\frac{\dfrac{\partial U^e / \partial \pi}{U^e(\pi)}}{\dfrac{\partial U^u / \partial B}{U^u(B)}} = 1, \qquad (2.1')$$

which implies that π and B would be divided in the ratio of the elasticities of the two parties' rescaled utility functions:

$$\frac{\pi}{B} = \frac{(\partial U^e / \partial \pi)[\pi / U^e(\pi)]}{(\partial U^u / \partial B)[B / U^u(B)]}. \qquad (2.2)$$

More precisely, π and B would be divided in the ratio of the elasticities of the two parties' utility increments.

Luce and Raiffa [1957], p. 129, interpret this characteristic of the Nash solution as favoring the wealthier of the two players. They present an example in which a wealthy man has a linear utility function and a poor man has a utility function

11. In this case, $\partial \pi / \partial B = -1$.

the elasticity of which diminishes rapidly. If one assumes that all individuals have the same utility function but that different individuals are operating in different regions of the domain of the function, then one could easily conclude that the Nash solution is likely to favor the poor man. If the universal utility function displays declining elasticity (as does a quadratic for instance), the elasticity in the poor man's region will be greater than the elasticity in the rich man's region.

The efficiency axiom is satisfied because the solution lies on the utility frontier, and the symmetry axiom is satisfied because if the utility increments frontier were symmetric, the two elasticities would be equal and the total sum of money would be divided evenly between the two parties. It is easy to see that a linear transformation of the utility functions would leave the elasticity of each utility increment function unchanged, and therefore transformation invariance is satisfied. Finally, independence of irrelevant alternatives is satisfied because any restriction of the utility frontier which left the solution point and the slope of the frontier at that point unchanged would leave the elasticities unchanged.[12]

2.4.
Alternative Bargaining Theories

Nash's theory is far from being the only bargaining theory in the literature. Some of the alternative treatments of the bargaining problem are also based on game theory, and others have independent origins. Raiffa is the author of three game-theoretic solutions of the fixed-threat bargaining problem[13] and Bishop has proposed another.[14] Two of Raiffa's solutions satisfy the axioms of efficiency, symmetry, and transformation invariance, and thus differ from Nash only in the rejection of the independence of irrelevant alter-

12. Nash's proof is set theoretic in nature and does not depend on the existence of the slope of the utility frontier.
13. See Raiffa [1953] and Luce and Raiffa [1957], p. 137.
14. See Bishop [1963], pp. 572–574.

natives axiom. (Bishop rejects the transformation invariance assumption.)

Still greater is the number of bargaining theories not related to game theory. However, interestingly enough, most of these imply solutions that are either always identical with Nash's solution or that agree with Nash's solution in special cases.

The first determinate solution to the bargaining problem ever proposed was originally stated by the Danish economist Zeuthen in *Problems of Monopoly and Economic Warfare* in 1928[15] and subsequently refined by Harsanyi [1956]. Both Zeuthen and Harsanyi transform the bargaining problem into a problem of risk and apply to it the techniques of maximization of expected utility. Let the two opponents be again "e" and "u", and let the utility to each of the outcome be U^e and U^u. Arbitrarily scale these utilities so that each party obtains zero utility if there is a stalemate. Assume that "e" opens the negotiations with an initial offer that would give him U^{ee} and his opponent U^{ue}, whereas "u" opens with an offer that would give him U^{uu} and his opponent U^{eu}. Typical initial offers are represented in Fig. 2.2.

The Zeuthen–Harsanyi approach consists of assuming that each party is continually comparing the alternatives of immediately accepting his opponent's latest offer versus holding out for his current demand, at the risk of causing a stalemate. If "e", for instance, accepts his opponent's offer, he obtains U^{eu}. If he holds out, his expected utility is $(1 - p)U^{ee}$, where p is the probability that there will be a stalemate. Zeuthen and Harsanyi define e's "propensity to fight" as the maximum probability of a stalemate

---

15. This was translated into English in 1930. See Zeuthen [1930], especially chapter 4.

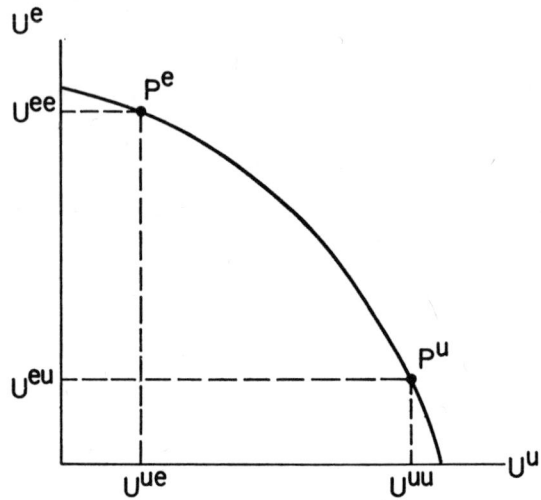

Figure 2.2. The Demands of the Two Parties in a Zeuthen–Harsanyi Game

he is willing to endure in order to obtain his demand. This is the value of p which equates $(1 - p)U^{ee}$ with U^{eu}, i.e., $(U^{ee} - U^{eu})/U^{ee}$.

Agreement is obtained through an atonement process whereby the party with the lowest propensity to fight always reduces his demand. Harsanyi proved that the limit of this process is the point where $U^e U^u$ is a maximum. Since the two utilities have been scaled in such a way as to place the threat point at the origin, the Zeuthen–Harsanyi solution is the same as the Nash solution.[16]

Another group of bargaining theories traces its origins to Chapter 7 of Hicks' *Theory of Wages* (1963), in which the author argues that

---

16. Several other authors have approached the bargaining problem as a problem of risk, e.g., Pen [1952, 1959], Saraydar [1965], Schackle [1949], Stevens [1963], and Walton and McKensie [1965], to name only some of them. In general, the models of these theorists are not determinate in the sense that they do not definitely predict the outcome of negotiations. Another bargaining theory of a somewhat different type is that of Chamberlain [1955].

both the employer's tendency to make concessions and the union's resistance are a function of the expected duration of a strike. Several authors have constructed complete bargaining theories from the elements sketched roughly by Hicks, one of the analytically clearest and simplest being that of Foldes [1964].

The essence of Foldes' approach is that disagreement involves delay. "It is assumed that trade cannot begin (or that there will be a 'strike') until agreement is reached . . . and that any delay will diminish the utility of both parties."[17] It is again best explained by means of an example. As in the Nash example, let the two opponents "e" and "u" bargain over the distribution of a fixed quantity of money, e's share being called π and u's, B. The utility to each of a settlement depends now not only on the amount he receives but also on the time when the settlement occurs. Let these utilities be $U^e(\pi, t)$ and $U^u(B, t)$, with t the time the agreement is reached. (Negotiations begin at time zero.)

Assume that "e" opens with an initial demand of π^e (offering his opponent B^e), and "u" opens with a demand of B^u (offering π^u). Foldes defines each party's "delay time" as the maximum delay he would be willing to endure in order to obtain his current demand rather than his opponent's latest offer. Therefore at the outset, e's delay time is the value of t which satisfies $U^e(\pi^e, t) = U^e(\pi^u, 0)$. Foldes then argues that the two parties will agree to divide the total sum of money in such a way that if either tried to press for more the other would have a longer delay time and would threaten to hold out for longer. He proves that, in this simple case, this is the point where

$$\frac{\partial U^e/\partial \pi}{\partial U^e/\partial t} = \frac{\partial U^u/\partial B}{\partial U^u/\partial t}.$$

17. Foldes [1964], p. 120.

Sufficient conditions for the existence of such a point are that the indifference curves of the two parties (which represent the trade-off between goods and delay) be everywhere strictly concave and that all marginal rates of substitution be independent of time.

A case of special interest is that of constant rates of time discount: $U^e = f^e(\pi)e^{-at}$ and $U^u = f^u(B)e^{-bt}$. In this case, at the Foldes solution,

$$\frac{f^{e'} f^u}{f^{u'} f^e} = \frac{a}{b};$$

hence,

$$\frac{\dfrac{\partial U^e/\partial \pi}{U^e}}{\dfrac{\partial U^u/\partial B}{U^u}} = \frac{a}{b}. \qquad (2.3)$$

If the rates of time discount are equal, this condition is the same as that of Eq. 2.1′, which defines the Nash solution.

In the case which is the subject of this study, that is, in bargaining between an employer and a union, there is no reason to expect the rates of discount to differ; therefore the Foldes solution will be the same as the Nash solution. Even if the employer's and the union's rates of time discount were known to differ, the Foldes solution would be very similar to the Nash solution, the difference being only a proportionality constant.

Bishop [1964], Coddington [1966, 1968], and Cross [1965, 1966] have developed other bargaining theories that are also in the spirit of Hicks' original suggestions. The outcome of negotiations in Bishop's model coincides with the Foldes solution. Cross's model also leads to the Foldes solution in special cases. His contribution is the most ambitious of these. He does not assume perfect knowledge, and focuses attention on a dynamic learning process.

19 Alternative Bargaining Theories

If one considers the diverse motivations of the bargaining theories associated with Zeuthen, Hicks, and Nash, it is remarkable that they should lead to solutions that are so similar, if not identical. The firm basis of Nash's solution in game theory makes it the most satisfying version of the three. There is something *ad hoc* about both the Zeuthen assumption that bargaining strength is simply a function of the ability to endure risk and the Hicksian assumption that it is simply a function of ability to endure delay. By contrast, the derivation of Nash's theory from formal axioms concerning the behavior of rational individuals in situations of conflict involves at least an attempt to reach first principles.

If its game-theoretic foundations make Nash's theory preferable to those derived from Zeuthen and Hicks, the similarity of its conclusions and those of the latter gives it the edge over Raiffa's alternative game-theoretic solutions. It was this consideration plus the reasonably instinctive appeal of the axiom of independence of irrelevant alternatives—the axiom that separates Nash's solution from Raiffa's two prime contenders—which suggested the choice of Nash's theory as the basis for this study.

This being said, the importance of minor differences between otherwise similar theories should not be overemphasized, because any one of them would probably suffice for our purposes.

Suppose that whenever an employer and a union approach a bargaining situation in which their demands are consistent, and they know it, they reach an agreement. If they find the agreement by appealing to some accepted rule as to how to divide the gains from trade, and if any such accepted rule follows at least the first three axioms of Nash, it would follow that if different collective bargaining units chose somewhat different rules, the differences would not be great. For instance, whenever the utility frontier is a straight line, the solution will always be at the midpoint.

Now suppose that every collective bargaining unit in an industry is consistent in its choice of rule from one bargain to the next. Then, if the composition of units in the industry does not change markedly, the relationship between the size of settlements and economic conditions in the industry will be stable over time. Because admissible rules do not differ markedly from one another, it will not be misleading to deduce hypotheses about this relationship from any particular member of the family of admissible rules. Thus, even if Nash's theory did not describe every contract negotiation perfectly, even if some units followed the Nash pattern while others followed Zeuthian or Hicksian patterns, a set of equations derived from Nash's theory could still provide a reasonable explanation of the determination of wages and other variables in the industry.

2.5.
Summary

It is perhaps appropriate that this chapter end with a statement of what Nash's theory is not. It is not a theory of strikes. If employers and unions always behaved as Nash's theory predicts, there never would be a strike. It would be desirable to have an integrated theory that explained strikes and their duration as well as the characteristics of agreements when they occur. The beginnings of such a theory may lie in the relaxation of the assumption of perfect knowledge. The work of Cross [1965] is an important step in this direction.[18] However, as his work shows, such a theory must be very complex.

18. See also the study of strike activity by Ashenfelter and Johnson [1969].

3

A Nash Model of Bilateral Monopoly

3.1.
Introduction

To obtain a wage equation for a single employer and a single union, one must first derive a complete model of the firm under bilateral monopoly, with equations for employment, capital stock, output, price, and profits as well as wages. Such a model is derived in this chapter.

3.2.
Assumptions

Assume that the employer produces a good X whose demand curve is

$$P = P(X; \mathscr{P}, \mathscr{X}), \tag{3.1}$$

where P is the price of X, $\mathscr{P}$ is a general price index, and $\mathscr{X}$ is aggregate income. The long-run production function

$$X = X(E, K; t) \tag{3.2}$$

is twice differentiable and convex. (E is the number of workers and K the capital stock.) In the short run the supply of capital is fixed. In the long run it is infinitely elastic at the rental R.

All of the employees belong to one union, which obtains its members in infinitely elastic supply at the going wage rate from nonunionized industries. Dunlop has called such a supply function the "membership function."[1] The going wage rate in the relevant nonunionized industries is W^a.

Assume that both the employer and the union have utility functions that are unique up to an order-preserving, linear trans-

1. See Dunlop [1944], Chapter 3.

formation. The two most important assumptions of this study are those concerning the arguments of the utility functions of both the employer and the union. The employer's utility is a function of monopoly profits, i.e., profits net of a normal return on capital,

$$\pi \equiv PX - WE - RK, \tag{3.3}$$

where W is the union wage rate. Moreover, it is a linear function of monopoly profits, because the employer is a strict profit maximizer:

$$U^e = \alpha_0 + \alpha_1 \pi. \tag{3.4}$$

Let the union's utility function be a function of the difference between the real wage bill and what the real wage bill would be if its members earned nonunion wages. If we let B represent this difference, then

$$U^u = \beta_0 + \beta_1 f^u(B);^2 \qquad f^{u'} > 0; f^{u''} \leq 0; \tag{3.5}$$

$$B = \frac{WE - W^a E}{\mathscr{P}}. \tag{3.6}$$

B shall be referred to as the real "wage surplus."

The assumption that the union's utility is a function of the real wage surplus is more novel and therefore more difficult to justify than the assumption that the employer is a profit maximizer. The very notion that the aims of the union can be expressed solely in terms of economic variables has been a subject of ongoing debate between labor economists. The view of Ross [1956] and others is that the union can only be understood as a complex political institution. The opposing position, stated by Dunlop [1944] and

2. The parameters β_0 and β_1 are unobservable, arbitrary constants that reflect the indistinguishability of the utility function from linear transformations of itself.

others, is that the union is primarily an economic organization whose aims economists should analyze in much the same way as they analyze other economic agents.

One of the hypotheses advanced by Dunlop was that the union's utility is a function of the wage bill, WE. This represented an improvement over earlier treatments in which the union was presented as interested solely in maximizing the wage rate, because some weight was also given to employment. But the hypothesis was still unsatisfactory because it implied the union's willingness to lower its wage indefinitely in order to increase employment.[3] The wage-surplus hypothesis is an extension of the wage-bill hypothesis which is not susceptible to that criticism. A union maximizing its wage surplus would never be willing to lower its wage below the supply price of labor, W^a. The basic rationale for the wage-surplus hypothesis is that it makes the union's utility a function of that part of the wage bill which is union induced. In technical terms, the union is treated as if it were the monopolist of an intermediate product whose cost is W^a.[4]

Finally, assume that the monopoly profits and wage surplus expected by the employer and the union if they withdraw from the industry are π^0 and B^0, respectively.

3.3.
A Model of the Firm

As shown in Chapter 2, Nash's theory of fixed-threat bargaining implies that the two parties will reach an agreement on their

---
3. This drawback of the wage bill hypothesis has been pointed out by Rees [1963], p. 53.
4. The assumption that the union's objective is to maximize its monopoly rents has been used similarly to the way it is used here by Rosen [1969, 1970].

contract curve, and that this will be at a point that corresponds to unitary elasticity of the utility increments frontier.

Though the statement that the agreement lies on the contract curve has long been accepted in the general literature on bargaining, its application to employer–union negotiations requires some discussion. One popular view of collective bargaining is that all the employer and the union negotiate about is the wage rate and that the employer adjusts employment, capital stock, output, and particularly prices to changes in wages in such a way as to maximize profits. This implies that every agreement eventually places the employer and the union on the long-run demand curve for labor rather than on the contract curve. The rationale for this view is, of course, that wages and working conditions are the principal subject matter of labor contracts. What this view misses is, on the one hand, the fact that the strike threat indirectly gives the union a voice in all the activities of the employer and, on the other, that limitation of possible outcomes to points on the long-run demand curve for labor is not efficient from either the employer's or the union's point of view. Only on the contract curve is it true that each party's utility is a maximum, given his opponent's utility.

It will be assumed here that the employer and the union do reach the contract curve, and that the way they reach it is through implicit agreement on nonwage issues. Some form of agreement on W and E is necessary, the reason being that these are the two variables in the union's utility function that are affected by the employer's actions. However, the agreement on E need not deal directly with E but may be in the form of an implicit agreement on P and K, which together determine E. Framing the issue in this manner renders more acceptable the assumption that the outcome lies on the contract curve, for, though an implicit agreement concerning the level of employment seems unlikely, an understanding concerning pricing policy and capital-expansion plans is plausible, particularly in view of ever-increasing demands on the part of unions for information concerning the operation of the firm. One famous case in the United States in which an understanding concerning pricing policy does seem to have been an implicit part of the contract is the 1962 steel agreement.

If the outcome of every negotiation between an employer and a union is located on the contract curve, then derivation of the contract curve becomes an important first step in the construction of a bilateral monopoly model. Given the assumptions we outlined concerning utility, the characteristics of the contract curve are very simple to describe. On it, employment and capital stock are at the levels that a simple monopolist facing the same opportunity costs would have chosen. This can be shown as follows: The union is interested in maximizing $(WE - W^a E)/\mathscr{P}$. Given $\mathscr{P}$, which the union cannot influence, this amounts to maximizing $WE - W^a E$. The employer on the other hand is interested in maximizing

$$\pi = PX - WE - RK = PX - W^a E - RK - (WE - W^a E).$$

The joint interest of the two parties consists of maximizing the sum of these two objectives, $PX - W^a E - RK$; this is exactly what a monopolist who purchased labor and capital at the fixed rates W^a and R would do. Therefore E and K are determined by the traditional first-order conditions

$$\left(P + \frac{\partial P}{\partial X} X\right) \frac{\partial X}{\partial E} = W^a, \tag{3.7}$$

$$\left(P + \frac{\partial P}{\partial X} X\right) \frac{\partial X}{\partial K} = R, \tag{3.8}$$

which, along with Eqs. 3.1 and 3.2, also determine X and P. The only variable free to move on the contract curve is W. In other words, movement to the contract curve can be viewed as a maximization of the joint surplus of employer and union. All that remains for them to do is to divide this surplus by fixing the wage rate.[5]

It is the unit elasticity condition that determines the distribution of net revenue between the two parties. The expression for that condition can be obtained simply by extending the example of Nash's theory given in Chapter 2, in which "e" and "u" were assumed to have utilities $U^e(\pi)$ and $U^u(B)$, respectively, and π was assumed to be a function of B along the contract curve: $\pi = \pi(B)$, $(d\pi/dB) < 0$. The solution in that case was at the point where Eq. 2.1 (p. 12) holds. In this case the relation $\pi(B)$ has a very simple form because of the constancy of net revenue,

$$PX - W^a E - RK = \pi + \mathscr{P}B.$$

In fact, it is easy to see that

$$\frac{d\pi}{dB} = -\mathscr{P}.$$

Substituting this and Eqs. 3.4 and 3.5 into Eq. 2.1, one obtains

$$\frac{\mathscr{P}/(\pi - \pi^0)}{\dfrac{\partial f^u/\partial B}{f^u(B) - f^u(B^0)}} = 1.$$

This can be shown, by rearranging terms, to be equivalent to

$$\frac{WE - W^a E}{\pi} = \frac{\pi - \pi^0}{\pi} \frac{(\partial f^u/\partial B)B}{f^u(B) - f^u(B^0)}. \tag{3.9}$$

---

5. This discussion of joint maximization by the employer and the union is a restatement of the classical analysis of bilateral monopoly by Fellner [1947].

This equation determines the distribution of income between the employer and the union. In words, the wage surplus and profits are divided in proportion to the elasticities of the incremental utility functions of the two parties.

Equation 3.9, along with the profit identity, Eq. 3.3, completes the Nash model of bilateral monopoly, which consists thus of those two equations and Eqs. 3.1, 3.2, 3.7, and 3.8, which together determine P, X, E, K, W, and π. In fact, the model is decomposable; i.e., Eqs. 3.1, 3.2, 3.7, and 3.8 determine P, X, E, and K as a function of $\mathscr{P}$, $\mathscr{X}$, t, W^a, and R. Then Eqs. 3.9 and 3.3 determine W and π as a function of P, X, E, and K plus π^0 and B^0. If the profit identity is substituted into Eq. 3.9, this equation then determines W directly as a function of P, X, E, K, π^0, and B^0. It is therefore natural to view Eq. 3.9 as the wage equation whose derivation essentially motivated the construction of the model.

3.4.
Summary
Nash's theory of bargaining has been applied to a very simple, static model of bilateral monopoly between one employer and one union. The derivation of its equations brought out two fundamental characteristics of collective bargaining. One is that collective bargaining is more than a question of wages and working conditions. The ability of the union to veto by means of a strike any action of the employer calls the entire theory of the firm into question and necessitates its reconstruction from new assumptions. In the Nash model the union is actually in the product market along with the employer.[6]

---

6. Contrasts should not be overemphasized. As will be seen in the next chapter, the new model actually bears much resemblance to the standard simple-monopoly model.

The second point—which is common knowledge, but which this chapter reemphasizes—is that the interests of the employer and the union are not in conflict in all of the areas of activity of the firm. In this model, their common interest encompasses capital plans, the determination of employment, and pricing policy. This is a fact which the game-theoretic treatment of bargaining on which this chapter is based emphasizes, highlighting, as it does, the non-zero-sum nature of employer–union relations.

4

Comparative Statics of the Nash Model

4.1.
Introduction

Any model is only as interesting as the facts it explains. As a prelude to the empirical validation of the Nash model of bilateral monopoly in subsequent chapters, this chapter will examine its comparative static properties. First the Nash model will be compared with the standard simple-monopoly model; then the effect on the firm's decision variables in the model—in particular on W—of changes in two strategically important exogenous variables will be examined: the profits tax and the general price level.

4.2.
Bilateral Monopoly and Monopoly Contrasted

Though the basic assumptions of the Nash model and the standard model of a monopolist facing a competitive labor market are quite different, their behavioral equations are very similar. In fact, a simple version of the standard monopoly model could be constructed from the first four behavioral equations (Eqs. 3.1, 3.2, 3.7, and 3.8) and the profits identity (Eq. 3.3) of Nash's model. The only difference between the standard monopoly model and the Nash model is the presence of Eq. 3.9, corresponding to the presence of an additional variable. In the Nash model there are two wage variables, W and W^a. When the monopolist faces a competitive labor market, $W = W^a$. This means that the movements of P, X, E, and K are exactly the same in the Nash model as they would be in the model with a competitive labor market. In short, the union does not alter the allocation of resources.

What is different is the distribution of income. It is easy to see that the Nash model separates the distribution of income from the allocation of resources by noting that neither the product-demand curve nor the production function appear in any way on the right-hand side of Eq. 3.9. Distribution is determined by the firm's own wage W, whereas factor demand and output decisions are based on the supply price of labor to the union. In general, the labor share is greater in the Nash model than in the model with a competitive labor market. Consider again the wage equation, 3.9. All the terms on its right-hand side are positive. Therefore, if π is also positive, $W > W^a$. There are two exceptions to this. One occurs when net revenue is temporarily negative. If $PX < W^aE + RK$, then Eq. 3.9 dictates that the union will share the losses. The value of W will be such that $W < W^a$ and $PX < WE + RK$.

The other exception is the limiting case of perfect competition in the product market. If the employer is a perfect competitor, then in the long run $PX = W^aE + RK$, and therefore $W = W^a$. In general, the employer and the union share the surplus of revenue over competitive wage costs and capital costs. If the product market is perfectly competitive, there is no long-run surplus to share.

The proof that under perfect competition in the long run $W = W^a$ follows: The right-hand side of Eq. 3.9 is strictly positive in the long run (for otherwise the firm would go out of business), but finite. If the firm is a perfect competitor, $\pi = 0$; therefore $W = W^a$, for otherwise the left-hand side of Eq. 3.9 could not be finite.

This implication of the Nash model agrees very well with a recurrent theme in the labor-economics literature. Labor economists have long argued that the influence of product-market force on the wage rate is greater in unionized than in nonunionized industry.[1] Dunlop [1944] was one of the first to make this argument. The hypothesis has stimulated much empirical research on the subject

1. For a critique of this argument, see Rees [1963], p. 83.

of the relation between profits and wages and/or product-market concentration and wages.[2] The Nash model explains in a precise manner what the relationship between the product market and the wage rate in a unionized industry is and how it differs from the same relationship in an industry with a competitive labor market. The notion is that the union shares the monopoly profits of the firm with the employer.

With this perspective on the general characteristics of the Nash model, the ground is now prepared for analysis of the effects of a profits tax and of changes in the general price level on P, X, E, K, and π.

4.3.
Forward Shifting of a Profits Tax

Whether or not the U.S. corporate profits tax is shifted, and if so, by how much, is an issue that has been debated and studied for a long time. Classical price theory says that a tax on net profits has no effect on price, output, employment, or wages in the short run. But it has been argued by some that corporations raise their prices in the short run in response to the tax and by others that they pay lower wages in response to the tax. Perry [1966] in particular has argued that in manufacturing industries an increase in the U.S. corporate income tax would reduce wage increases. The empirical evidence to date[3] suggests that, whatever the effects on prices and wages are, they may cancel out and leave before-tax profits unchanged. Unfortunately, this leaves unresolved the question of what actually happens to prices and wages.

2. See Bowen [1960], Levinson [1960], Perry [1966], and Weiss [1966], among others.
3. R. J. Gordon [1967] reversed the previous conclusions of Kryzaniak and Musgrave [1963]. See also the comment and reply by Gordon [1968].

In this section and the next the issue of long-run shifting will be bypassed, because the Nash model has nothing new to contribute to the analysis. Operationally this means the profits tax will be assumed to leave K unchanged.

What will be done is first to show that neither output, employment, nor price is changed in the short run by any tax on monopoly profits. This amounts simply to a review of standard short-run price theory. In addition it will be shown in Section 4.4 that a linear tax on monopoly profits leaves the wage rate unchanged in the model and that a progressive tax will tend to cause the wage rate to be higher, not lower, than it otherwise would have been. It will be argued that in the short run, when RK is fixed, the U.S. corporate income tax can be viewed roughly as a linear tax on monopoly profits. Therefore the model does not support the Perry hypothesis.

Let $T(\pi)$ be a tax on monopoly profits and $D(\pi) = \pi - T(\pi)$ be monopoly profits after tax. Assume $0 < D'(\pi) < 1$. The first step is to show that a tax on profits leaves the optimal level of employment in the short run unchanged. The reason is simple. After-tax profits are a monotonic, increasing function of before-tax profits. Therefore, the level of E that maximizes before-tax profits also maximizes after-tax profits. In the short run, P and X are solely functions of E. Therefore, they are also unaffected by a profits tax.

4.4.
Backward Shifting of a Profits Tax

Ascertaining the effect of a profits tax on the wage rate is more difficult. The only behavioral equation out of the five in the Nash model affected by the tax is the wage equation. Therefore, a good place to begin the analysis is with the derivation of the wage equation for the case when there is a profits tax. Each variable that might be different in a tax world from what it is in a no-tax world will be represented in the following manner: W and B in a tax world will be $\tilde{W}$ and $\tilde{B}$, and before-tax profits in a tax world will be $\tilde{\pi}$.

Once again the easiest way to derive the unit elasticity condition —which is the original form of the wage equation—is by extension of the Nash example in Chapter 2. In this case, since the employer's utility is a function of after-tax profits, $U^e[D(\pi)]$, the analog of the contract curve relation $\pi(B)$ is $D[\pi(B)]$, whose derivative is $(\partial D/\partial \pi)(d\pi/dB)$. It was shown in Chapter 3 that $d\pi/dB = -\mathscr{P}$; therefore, the derivative of $D[\pi(B)]$ is $-(\partial D/\partial \pi)\mathscr{P}$. The utility increments frontier is unit elastic when (see Eq. 2.1, p. 12)

$$\frac{\dfrac{\partial D/\partial \pi}{D(\tilde{\pi}) - D(\pi^0)}}{\dfrac{\partial f^u/\partial B}{f^u(\tilde{B}) - f^u(B^0)}} = 1. \tag{4.1}$$

Rearranging of terms changes this to

$$\frac{\tilde{W}E - W^aE}{\tilde{\pi}} = \frac{D(\tilde{\pi}) - D(\pi^0)}{(\partial D/\partial \pi)\tilde{\pi}} \frac{(\partial f^u/\partial B)\tilde{B}}{f^u(\tilde{B}) - f^u(B^0)}. \tag{4.2}$$

Comparing this equation with Eq. 3.9, one sees that if $(D - D^0)/[(\partial D/\partial \pi)\pi] = (\pi - \pi^0)/\pi$; then $\tilde{\pi} = \pi$, $\tilde{B} = B$, and the solution is the same as in a no-tax world. This condition can be rewritten

$$\frac{\partial D}{\partial \pi} = \frac{D - D^0}{\pi - \pi^0}.$$

It is then easy to see that the only tax for which this will be true is a linear tax,

$$T = a + b\pi.$$

Thus, a linear tax leaves B and W unchanged. The fact that this result holds for any linear tax, not just any proportional tax, means that it holds in the short run for any tax with a constant marginal rate, regardless of whether or not it is also levied on a portion of capital costs, RK, as the U.S. corporate income tax is. Since, moreover, the marginal rate of the latter is roughly constant, the result holds for that tax. (Of course, in the long run, taxation of RK can have a significant effect on accumulation and thus can affect wages, prices, and other variables indirectly.)

If $T(\pi)$ is not linear, the situation is somewhat more complicated. If

$$\frac{D - D^0}{(\partial D/\partial \pi)\pi} \gtreqless \frac{\pi - \pi^0}{\pi},$$

then $\tilde{\pi}$ and $\tilde{B}$ differ from π and B and the differences must be such as to insure that

$$\frac{\widetilde{W}E - W^aE}{\tilde{\pi}} \cdot \frac{f^u(\tilde{B}) - f^u(B^0)}{(\partial f^u/\partial B)\tilde{B}} \gtreqless \frac{WE - W^aE}{\pi} \cdot \frac{f^u(B) - f^u(B^0)}{(\partial f^u/\partial B)B}.$$

Therefore, there are two steps to considering the effect of a non-proportional tax on B. First one must consider whether or not

$$\frac{D - D^0}{(\partial D/\partial \pi)\pi} \gtreqless \frac{\pi - \pi^0}{\pi}.$$

Next one must ask whether

$$\frac{d}{dB}\left[\frac{\mathscr{P}B}{\pi} \frac{f^u(B) - f^u(B^0)}{(\partial f^u/\partial B)B}\right] \gtreqless 0.$$

It is simplest to answer the second question first, since its answer is independent of the type of tax:

$$\frac{d}{dB}\left[\frac{\mathscr{P}B}{\pi}\frac{f^u(B)-f^u(B^0)}{(\partial f^u/\partial B)B}\right] = \frac{f^u(B)-f^u(B^0)}{(\partial f^u/\partial B)B}\left(\frac{\pi+B}{\pi^2}\right)\mathscr{P}$$
$$+ \frac{B}{\pi}\frac{d}{dB}\left[\frac{f^u(B)-f^u(B^0)}{(\partial f^u/\partial B)B}\right]\mathscr{P}.$$

The first term is > 0. The second is proportional to the derivative of the inverse of the elasticity of the union's incremental utility function; it is nonnegative if and only if the latter has a nonincreasing elasticity. The following three conditions are sufficient for this to be the case:

$B^0 = 0$;

$f^u(0) = 0$;

$\frac{d}{dB}\left(\frac{\partial f^u}{\partial B}\frac{B}{f^u}\right) \leq 0.$

The first condition holds if the earnings of union members in their best alternative activity are, in fact, determined by the going wage in nonunionized industry. The second and third conditions involve the form of the union's utility function. Examples of functions that satisfy them include linear and constant-elastic functions. It is easy to demonstrate that under these conditions

$$\frac{d}{dB}\left[\frac{f^u(B)-f^u(B^0)}{(\partial f^u/\partial B)B}\right] > 0.$$

It follows that

$$\frac{d}{dB}\left[\frac{\mathscr{P}B}{\pi}\frac{f^u(B)-f^u(B^0)}{(\partial f^u/\partial B)B}\right] > 0,$$

and therefore any tax that causes

$$\frac{D - D^0}{(\partial D/\partial \pi)\pi} > \frac{\pi - \pi^0}{\pi}$$

will cause B, and thus W, to rise. All that remains to be asked is what taxes will bring about this condition. One important category of taxes that have this effect is clearly that of all strictly progressive taxes, that is, taxes for which $(\partial^2 D/\partial \pi^2) < 0$ for all positive values of π.[4] In short, if the elasticity of the union's incremental utility function is either constant or a diminishing function of B, a strictly progressive tax on monopoly profits will cause W to be higher than it otherwise would have been. In lieu of a summary, one may now recapitulate the first conclusion of this section: Regardless of the form of the union's utility function, a linear tax on monopoly profits leaves the wage rate unchanged.

4.5.
Money Wages and the General Price Level

The elasticity of the money wage rate with respect to the general price level has been a troubled issue in earlier analyses of money wage determination. Attention has been focused on whether or not theory leads to the expectation that the money wage in a particular market be homogeneous of degree one in all other wages and prices. A particularly unsettled issue is the relevance of Phillips curve studies, such as those of Hansen [1951], Phillips [1958], Lipsey [1960], and many others, to this question.

[4]. The condition in question may be rewritten $\partial D/\partial \pi < (D - D^0)/(\pi - \pi^0)$. This condition is met if $\partial^2 D/\partial \pi^2 < 0$, because then $\partial D/\partial \pi$ is smaller than the tangent of a secant between D and any point corresponding to a $D^0 < D$.

In the Nash model, the cost of living plays a minor role. The main influence of changes in the general price level is through other channels. But—and this is the important point—these channels are such that the money wage in a unionized industry will be homogeneous of degree one in all other wages and prices in the economy.

Suppose that W^a, R, π^0, B^0, and $\mathscr{P}$ all rise equiproportionally. Since the Nash model is decomposable, the study of the effects of these changes can be undertaken in two stages: the effects on E, K, X, and P first, and on W and π second. The former depend on the shape of the product demand curve, Eq. 3.1. If P is homogeneous of degree one in $\mathscr{P}$, then the marginal revenue product is also homogeneous of degree one in $\mathscr{P}$, and the left-hand sides of Eqs. 3.7 and 3.8 (the labor and capital demand equations) rise in proportion to $\mathscr{P}$. Since, by assumption, the right-hand sides also rise in proportion, E and K, and therefore also X, remain unchanged.

Given the constancy of E, K, and X, the effect of the postulated changes on W and π depends on the wage equation and the profits identity, Eqs. 3.9 and 3.3. It is easy to show that if $\mathscr{P}$, W^a, R, π^0, and B^0 all rise equiproportionally, W and π must rise in the same proportion to preserve equality in Eqs. 3.9 and 3.3. This proves that W is homogeneous of degree one in W^a, R, π^0, B^0, and $\mathscr{P}$.

Constancy of X and E implies that if W does change in proportion with P and R, π will also. Also, if W changes in proportion with $\mathscr{P}$, it follows that

$$B = \frac{(W - W^a)E}{\mathscr{P}}$$

will remain unchanged.

It will now be shown that W and π do rise in proportion with P, the proof being that these changes are consistent with Eqs. 3.9 and 3.3. Therefore, equiproportional increases in W and π represent a new equilibrium, which is unique (see p. 13). Let $\mathscr{P}$ increase. Then, X and E will remain unchanged, and P will rise by the same proportion as $\mathscr{P}$. By assumption, W^a will rise in the same proportion. Assume that W also rises in the same proportion. Then,

$$B = \frac{(W - W^a)E}{\mathscr{P}}$$

will remain unchanged. Also, the profit identity will require π to rise in the same proportion. But this is consistent with the distribution equation, because, if B is constant and W, W^a, and π rise in the same proportion, then

$$\frac{(\partial f^u/\partial B)B}{f^u(B) - f^u(B^0)}, \quad \frac{\pi - \pi^0}{\pi}, \quad \text{and} \quad \frac{(W - W^a)E}{\pi},$$

all remain unchanged. Thus increases in W and π of the same proportion as the increase in $\mathscr{P}$ do correspond to a new equilibrium.

The cost of living (that is, $\mathscr{P}$ in its role as a deflator for the union's money earnings) has played a minor role in the preceding argument. Its relatively secondary importance can be further underlined by demonstrating that, for a broad class of utility functions f^u, an equiproportional increase in P, W^a, R, π^0, and B^0 will cause W to rise in the same proportion, regardless of how $\mathscr{P}$ changes. The reason is that $\mathscr{P}$ acts like a proportional tax on B. And, by extension of the reasoning which proved that a proportional tax on profits leaves the wage rate unchanged, it can be shown that a proportional tax on B does not change the wage rate if f^u is a constant elastic function.

The only place where $\mathscr{P}$ appears in Eq. 3.9 is in the term

$$\frac{(\partial f^u/\partial B)B}{f^u(B) - f^u(B^0)},$$

because $B = (WE - W^a E)/\mathscr{P}$.

Of course neither the forgoing argument nor the preceding one implies anything about the behavior of W when W^a, R, π^0, and B^0 rise in different proportions. Thus it is clear that homogeneity of all wages in the economy to all prices depends crucially on the response of W^a to a general price increase.

4.6.
Summary

Comparative static analyses have been made of the effect on the distribution of income in the Nash model of (1) a profits tax and (2) an increase in the general price level. It was shown that both a linear tax on monopoly profits and an equiproportional increase in all exogenous prices leave the distribution of income unchanged.

5
A Testable Wage Equation

5.1.
Introduction

The aim of this chapter is to derive an empirically testable form for Eq. 3.9, the wage equation. of the Nash model. Even if the explanation of wages had not been the original objective of this study, the fact this is the single equation that differentiates the Nash model from the standard monopoly model would be reason enough to focus attention on it. For it follows that empirical validation of the equation, which is the subject of Chapters 6 and 7, is a test of the entire model.

5.2.
An Equilibrium Wage Equation

The wage equation, Eq. 3.9, can be considerably simplified with the help of one additional assumption. If one lets

$$\frac{\pi - \pi^0}{\pi} \frac{(\partial f^u/\partial B)B}{f^u(B) - f^u(B^0)} = \xi,$$

and substitutes the profit identity, Eq. 3.3, into Eq. 3.9, it becomes

$$W = \frac{\xi}{1 + \xi} \frac{PX - RK}{E} + \frac{1}{1 + \xi} W^a. \tag{5.1}$$

The wage rate is a weighted average of revenue net of capital costs per unit of labor and the going wage in nonunionized industry. Unfortunately the apparent simplicity of Eq. 5.1 is still somewhat misleading because ξ is itself a function of B, π, B^0, and π^0. However, if one assumes that $f^u(B)$ is linear, then

$$\xi = \frac{B/(B - B^0)}{\pi/(\pi - \pi^0)},$$

41 An Equilibrium Wage Equation

and the following approximation to Eq. 5.1 can be obtained:

$$W = \frac{1}{2}\left(\frac{PX - RK}{E}\right) + \frac{1}{2}W^a + c\frac{B^0}{B} - c\frac{\pi^0}{\pi}, \qquad (5.2)$$

where c is a parameter generated by the approximation, and $c > 0$. The equality of the coefficients of $(PX - RK)/E$ and W^a follows from the linearity of $f^u(B)$.

Equation 5.2 is obtained from Eq. 5.1 as follows:

$$dW = \left(\frac{\xi}{1+\xi}\right)d\left(\frac{PX-RK}{E}\right) + \frac{1}{1+\xi}dW^a + \left(\frac{PX-RK}{E} - W^a\right) \times \frac{1}{(1+\xi)^2}d\xi.$$

Furthermore, if

$$\xi = \frac{B/(B-B^0)}{\pi/(\pi-\pi^0)},$$

then,

$$d\xi = \left[\frac{B}{B-B^0}\frac{\pi^0}{\pi^2}\frac{d\pi}{dB} - \frac{\pi-\pi^0}{\pi}\frac{B^0}{(B-B^0)^2}\right]dB + \frac{\pi-\pi^0}{\pi}\frac{B}{(B-B^0)^2}dB^0 - \left(\frac{B}{B-B^0}\right)\frac{1}{\pi}d\pi^0.$$

Using these expressions for the relevant differentials, if one linearizes Eq. 5.1 around the sample averages $\overline{(PX-RK)/E}$ and $\overline{W^a}$ and the values $B^0 = 0$, $\pi^0 = 0$, one obtains Eq. 5.2. The parameter c is

$$c = \frac{1}{4}\left(\overline{\frac{PX-RK}{E}} - \overline{W^a}\right),$$

and it is likely that $\overline{(PX-RK)/E} > \overline{W^a}$.

It should be noted that $\mathscr{P}$ does not enter Eq. 5.2, as indeed it should not because a linear function is constant elastic, and it was shown in Section 4.5 that W is independent of $\mathscr{P}$—given P, W^a, R, π^0, and B^0—if $f^u(B)$ is constant elastic. Similarly, the corporate profits tax rate has not been entered because the tax has been assumed to be roughly equivalent to a linear tax on net profits and W was proved to be independent of such a tax in Section 4.4.

The simplicity of Eq. 5.2 is partly due to the decision to linearize in the neighborhood of the point where B^0 and π^0 are zero. This choice, however, also makes economic sense. B^0 and π^0 refer to the earnings which union members and employers expect they would receive if they withdrew from the industry. (B^0 is the excess of the union members' expected earnings over the going wage in nonunionized industry, and π^0 is the excess of the employer's expected profit over the competitive return to capital.) Since the supply price of labor to the union is the going wage in nonunionized industry, it is reasonable to expect B^0 to be close to zero. Similarly, the employer's expected profit in his best alternative is likely to be close to the competitive return to capital, and therefore π^0 is likely to be close to zero. It follows that $B^0 = \pi^0 = 0$ is a good choice of a point around which to linearize Eq. 5.1.

It should be emphasized, however, that linearizing a relationship around certain values of the independent variables in no way implies that the independent variables are identically equal to those values. The above arguments do not suggest that π^0 and B^0 are identically equal to zero, any more than $(PX - RK)/E$ and W^a are identically equal to their sample averages $\overline{(PX - RK)/E}$ and $\overline{W^a}$. In fact, both π^0 and B^0 can be expected to vary cyclically in such a way as to cause cyclical variation in W. The natural presumption is that both the union's and the employer's expectations of relative earnings in their best alternative activities improve with general business conditions because the variety of available alternatives increases. More importantly, it is also reasonable to assume that B^0/B is more sensitive to business conditions than π^0/π, first because the union is likely to discount the future more heavily than the employer and to be more interested in expectations of short-run alternatives, which in turn are likely to be particularly cyclically sensitive. The reason for the union discounting more heavily is that industrial turnover rates are so high that the average stay of a union member on any job is relatively short. Secondly, both union and employer may base their evaluations of earnings in alternative activities at least in part on the costs of a strike, and the union has relatively less to lose and more to gain from a strike when business conditions improve.

In the product market, if demand is low when a strike threatens, the employer is better capable of hedging against it. In industries that produce to stock, he can build up inventories before the strike. In industries that produce to order, he can let back orders accumulate during the strike and work them down afterwards. In either type of industry, if the employer faces several unions he can shift production during a strike to plants that are still operating.

On the other hand, in the labor market, if the demand for labor is generally high, union members are in a better position to hedge against the strike. The union's strike fund will be larger, it will be easier for striking members to find temporary jobs, and harder for the employer to replace them.

These arguments suggest replacing $B^0/B - \pi^0/\pi$ in Eq. 5.2 by some function of demand pressure. The assumption used here is

$$\frac{B^0}{B} - \frac{\pi^0}{\pi} = b_0 + b_1 N,$$

where N is some measure of demand pressure yet to be determined. Substitution into Eq. 5.2 gives

$$W = cb_0 + \frac{1}{2}\left(\frac{PX - RK}{E}\right) + \frac{1}{2}W^a + cb_1 N. \tag{5.3}$$

5.3.
Specification of Variables

Further specification of the variables on the right-hand side of Eq. 5.3—$(PX - RK)/E$, W^a, and N—is required if this equation is to serve as the basis for a test of the Nash model.

The first of these, $(PX - RK)/E$, is a form of net-value productivity per worker. It is significantly a long-run concept; that is, it refers to values of P, X, R, K, and E when the firm is in equilibrium and operating at full capacity. On the one hand, this fact simplifies the empirical representation of $(PX - RK)/E$ because it justifies the assumption that RK is proportional to PX, which in turn reduces the value productivity term to $(1 - \gamma) \times (PX/E)$.[1] On the other hand, however, it complicates the specification because long-run productivity X/E is in general not directly observable. However, if the long-run production function is known, it can be calculated. In Chapter 6 rough estimates of long-run productivity will be derived from a simple model of labor demand. Suffice it to say here that the model removes the effect of cyclical variations in the level of utilization from observed productivity.

The meaning of W^a (the supply price of labor to the union) is clear, but its measurement is difficult. The assumption used was that for each industry studied this supply price is determined by the average going wage in the low-wage, predominantly nonunionized sectors of the private economy, that is, wholesale and retail trade, services, and government enterprises.[2] The specific data series used was the only available quarterly series for these industries, an unpublished estimate of total compensation per man-hour constructed by the U.S. Bureau of Labor Statistics and Office of Business Economics. Several minor adjustments that were made are reported in Chapter 6 and the Data Appendix.

1. If capital is infinitely elastic at the rental rate R (see Chapter 3) and the long-run production function is Cobb–Douglas, $\gamma (PX/K) = R$, where γ is the product of the elasticity of output to capital and the ratio of marginal revenue to price.
2. The choice of industries to include in this sector is similar to that made by Lewis [1963] in his study of the union–nonunion wage differential. See especially Chapter 6.

Some of the arguments for introducing N in Eq. 5.3 refer to general conditions in the economy as a whole, others to conditions specific to the industry. However, in view of the likelihood of collinearity between two measures of demand pressure, it was decided to use only one and to let that be an industry-specific measure on the grounds that such a measure would reflect both industry-specific and general conditions. The measure chosen was the gross layoff rate, layoffs being defined as separations initiated by the employer because of general economic conditions.

Data were available for quits, layoffs, total separations, and total accessions. (Data for new hires are available only after 1958.) At first, both quits and layoffs were singled out for consideration because plots of their values suggested that there was more cyclical variation in their movement than in the movement of total accessions and total separations. (Quits are voluntary separations. An employee who leaves because he has been hired by another firm or because he is looking for another job quits.) Preliminary estimates of Eq. 5.6 indicated that quits and layoffs are highly correlated but that the layoff rate tended to give better fits. Consequently, the quit rate was eliminated in favor of the layoff rate for all subsequent estimation.

The choice of a turnover rate to measure labor demand pressure needs some explanation. One reason for choosing a turnover rate is that such rates are the only measures of labor demand pressure for which data are readily available by two-digit industry in the manufacturing sector since the Korean War. Quarterly unemployment rates for two-digit industries are not available before 1959.

However, even if unemployment data were available by two-digit industry, it would be of questionable validity. As is well known, unemployment by industry is defined as unemployment by industry of last attachment, which is a poor measure of an industry's available supply. In contrast, layoffs, which are gross additions to the pool of readily available workers, do measure this supply directly.

The use of turnover rates in industry wage studies has good precedent. Behman [1964, 1966, 1968] has demonstrated a strong empirical relationship between wage change and turnover rates. She has used the accessions rate, the rehire rate, the new hire rate, and the quit rate to explain wage change in the Manufacturing, Durable, and Nondurable aggregates and in individual two-digit industries.

The addition of turnover to unemployment—if not its substitution for unemployment—is suggested by some work by Cohen and Solow [1967]. They used the new hire rate and the unemployment rate to explain movements of help-wanted advertising. Help-wanted advertising can be viewed as a proxy for job vacancies. An excess demand theory of wage change would lead one to expect wage change to be related to job vacancies as well as unemployment.

5.4.
Dynamics of Adjustment

In one sense, the question of the timing of wage adjustments is very simple. Wages are adjusted when new contracts are negotiated. This fact suggests that the ideal data for testing the Nash model would have been individual contract data. However, the difficulty of collecting such data and the desire for generality motivated testing the model with data for two-digit manufacturing industries.

The question of timing is much more complicated when the universe to be explained consists of average wage rates in broad industries. In previous studies the problem has been handled in a number of different ways. Eckstein and Wilson [1962] divided the post-World War II period into wage rounds, periods demarcated by rough coincidence of contract negotiation and duration in key companies and unions. They then argued that the average wage change during each wage round depends on the average value of its determinants within that wage round. This gave them as many observations as there were wage rounds, of which from 1947 through 1960 there were four. Eckstein and Wilson used this approach to estimate wage equations for two-digit manufacturing industries and for an aggregate of highly unionized and concentrated industries which they called "the key group."

The approach of Perry [1966] is at the opposite pole both in specificity and in extent of disaggregation in time. He assumed that the duration of a contract in all bargaining units in the industrial aggregate is constant (one year) but that negotiations are spread evenly throughout the year. Therefore, each quarter the contracts covering one-fourth of the employees of the industry are being negotiated. This provides a rough justification for treating quarterly observations on the four-quarter rate of change of the average wage rate in the industry as independent observations. Relying on these assumptions, Perry used quarterly observations on overlapping four-quarter rates of change of the average wage as his basic data, obtaining thus close to fifty observations between the end of 1948 and the beginning of 1960. He applied this method to the manufacturing, durables, and nondurables aggregates. In subsequent studies, other economists have applied his method to the private, nonfarm economy on the one hand and to two-digit manufacturing industries on the other.[3]

Neither of these methods is ideal. The Eckstein–Wilson approach, relying heavily on wage rounds that are difficult to specify, may be

---

3. See Simler and Tella [1968] as an example of an aggregate study and Pierson [1968] as an example of a disaggregated study.

suspected of throwing away some information. The Perry approach does not account adequately for the impact of exceptionally large negotiations. Clearly, what is needed is a marriage of these two approaches. But just as clearly, this would require compilation of quarterly data on the frequency of negotiations by industry. Until such data become available, the best approach is a quarterly approach different from Perry's; this has been used by Kuh [1967] and Sargan [1964].

Both start with an equation for the equilibrium level of the wage rate in an industry. Equation 5.3 is similar to theirs. They then argue that the average wage in the industry moves a fraction of the way toward its equilibrium each quarter, implying that the greater the gap between the average wage in the industry and its equilibrium, the greater the change in the average. If one assumes static expectations, the equilibrium toward which the actual wage is always moving is the one corresponding to conditions of the recent past.

There are a number of motivations for a partial adjustment mechanism in this context: (1) This pattern might reflect a similar one in the individual bargaining units. Each time they negotiate, management and union representatives may attempt to close a fixed percentage of the ever-changing gap between their equilibrium wage and the current wage. (2) The number of firms determining wage increases may itself be an increasing function of the gap between the industry's average wage and its equilibrium. This could occur because of pressure on the part of unions to reopen wage negotiations before scheduled contract-expiration dates, or else because, in the nonunion portion of the industry, a widening gap increases the pressure for wage adjustments. (3) Between basic rate changes and during contracts, average wage rates may change as a result of deliberate job upgrading or other forms of drift.

Unlike Perry's specification, this dynamic pattern does not require the use of overlapping observations and it also permits clear identification of the equilibrium wage level.

The Kuh–Sargan distributed lag wage-adjustment mechanism has a simple algebraic representation. If one henceforth lets W represent the average wage rate in an industry and W^e the equilibrium toward which it is tending,

$$\Delta W_t = \lambda W_t^e - \lambda W_{t-1}. \tag{5.4}$$

Under the static expectations assumption, W^e may be represented by Eq. 5.3 lagged one-quarter (and modified as indicated in footnote 1):

$$\Delta W_t = \lambda c_0 + \tfrac{1}{2}\lambda(1-\gamma)\left(\frac{PX}{E}\right)_{t-1} + \tfrac{1}{2}\lambda W_{t-1}^a + \lambda c_1 N_{t-1} - \lambda W_{t-1}. \tag{5.5}$$

However, the static expectations assumption is unduly rigid. In particular, it is very likely that employers and unions do anticipate changes in W^e associated with changes in the general price level. In order to capture this expectations effect, the recent change in the cost-of-living index has been added to the right-hand side of Eq. 5.5. Even after this modification, the equation remains consistent with the proof in Section 4.6 that in equilibrium, under present assumptions, W is independent of the cost of living. The expectations effect which the change in the cost of living is intended to measure is a transient.

Implicit in the derivation of Eq. 5.5 was the assumption of no government intervention in the bargaining process, an assumption which clearly cannot be entertained without testing during the period when the Kennedy and Johnson administrations were placing political pressure on highly unionized industries to moderate wage settlements in line with the "guideposts." In order to test for the influence of the guideposts, a dummy variable G_t, equal to unity from 1962.2 through 1966.3 and zero elsewhere, was added to Eq. 5.5.

Finally, since all the variables except N in Eq. 5.5 are trend dominated, the equation was estimated in logarithmic form. This has the effect of transforming the dependent variable into the proportional rate of change of W.[4] The equation whose estimation will be reported in the following chapters is

$$\Delta \ln W_t = d_0 + \lambda d_1 \ln \left(\frac{PX}{E}\right)_{t-1} + \lambda d_2 \ln W^a_{t-1}$$
$$+ \lambda d_3 N_{t-1} - \lambda \ln W_{t-1} + d_4 \Delta \ln \mathscr{P}_{t-1} - d_5 G_t. \quad (5.6)$$

From Eq. 5.1 one can see that the steady-state elasticities of W to PX/E and W^a—d_1 and d_2—should be $\xi/(1 + \xi)[(PX - RK)/WE]$ and $1/(1 + \xi)(W^a/W)$, respectively. Their sum should always be unity and if, as was assumed, $f''(B)$ is linear and the average values of π^0 and B^0 are zero, their ratio should be as $[(PX - RK)/E]/W^a$.[5]

---

4. $\Delta \ln W_t \triangleq \dfrac{W_t - W_{t-1}}{W_{t-1}}$.

N was maintained as a natural value and not replaced by its logarithm, because it is not likely to be trend dominated.

5. In Eq. 5.3 the coefficients of $(PX - RK)/E$ and W^a are both 1/2 and their ratio is 1. The difference with Eq. 5.6 is that the latter is log-linear and that the relevant coefficients there are elasticities, not derivatives.

6

Wage Rates, Productivity, and Variable Construction

6.1. Introduction

Partly because of the constraints of data availability and partly out of a desire for macroeconomic applicability, it was decided to estimate Eq. 5.6 for manufacturing industries at the two-digit Standard Industrial Classification (S.I.C.) level of aggregation. It is clear that since the Nash model refers to bargaining between one employer and one union the equation had to be tested on highly unionized industries. In fact it was tested on industries in which the 1958 unionization rate was greater than 60 percent. The eight manufacturing industries that qualified and for which it was possible to obtain all the necessary data series are listed in Table 6.1. This chapter deals with several theoretical and empirical issues that arose in the process of construction of data series for the dependent and independent variables. References to data sources and listings of the constructed series appear in the Data Appendix.

Table 6.1. List of Industries in Study

Name of Industry	Standard Industrial Classification Number
Durable industries:	
Stone, clay, and glass products	32
Primary metal industries	33
Fabricated metal products	34
Machinery	35
Electrical equipment and supplies	36
Nondurable industries:	
Paper and allied products	26
Chemicals and allied products	28
Rubber and miscellaneous plastic products	30

6.2.
Wage Rates and Average Hourly Earnings

The dependent variable in Eq. 5.6 is the wage rate. But no comprehensive set of statistics exists on wage rates for the United States. The concept for which data are most readily available for individual industries within manufacturing is average hourly earnings of production workers. Movements in such earnings may diverge from movements in wage rates for a number of reasons:

1. The weights may change. The percentage of production-worker man hours accounted for by high-wage industries or establishments may vary, as may the percentage of man hours accounted for by high-grade labor within an establishment.

2. Movements in the hourly earnings of an individual worker may diverge from movements in his base wage rate because of changes in the amount of overtime as a percentage of total hours, changes in the amount of late-shift work as a percentage of total hours, changes in hours paid but not worked as a percentage of total, changes in his rating within a classification on a job ladder, and changes in his productivity if he is a piece-rate worker.

Some of these divergences can be viewed as changes in effective wage rates and thus should be retained for explanation. This is true of the upgrading of a worker in a job classification and of changes in the productivity of workers under piece rates. Upgrading is a means of responding to market pressures, and the productivity of piece-rate workers is an economic phenomenon like the level of the wage rate which one should be able to relate to variables such as productivity, alternative earnings, and labor demand.

Changes in effective wage rates due to changes in the ratio of hours paid to hours worked are probably a trend phenomenon.

Ignoring them is not likely to bias the results of a study of the cyclical movement of wage rates.

In the quarterly equations for the two-digit industries of this study, an attempt was made to account in a systematic way for the effect on average hourly earnings of interindustry shifts in man-hour weights and changes in average overtime hours. Changes in the amount of late-shift work as a percentage of total hours may be correlated with changes in overtime hours. This leaves changes in the average quality of employees as an important, cyclically sensitive variable whose effect on earnings it was not possible to account for.

The following notation will be used to explain the procedure used:

h^j = the average number of hours for which production workers were paid in a given week in plant j.

h^{sj} = the standard workweek in plant j.

$(h^j - h^{sj})^+$ = the average number of overtime hours for which each production worker in plant j was paid in a given week.

w^j = the average hourly earnings of production workers in plant j.

w^{sj} = the straight-time average hourly earnings of production workers in plant j.

$f^j = 1 + 0.5[(h^j - h^{sj})^+/h^j]$. If overtime is paid as if it were time and a half, and if all workers in the jth plant are receiving the same amount of overtime, $w^j = w^{sj}f^j$.

a^j = the share of production worker man-hours of the jth plant in total production worker man hours of its two-digit industry.

Assume that all production workers in any given plant work

equal hours and are paid at equal rates and that the standard workweek is the same at all plants in an industry, $h^{sj} = H^s$. For a given industry, the following identity holds,

$$W = \sum a^j w^j = \sum a^j w^{sj} f^j.$$

Therefore,

$$\dot{W} = \sum w^j \dot{a}^j + \sum a^j \dot{w}^j, \tag{6.1}$$

and

$$\frac{\dot{W}}{W} = \sum \frac{w^j}{W} \dot{a}^j + \sum \frac{a^j(w)^j}{W}\left(\frac{\dot{f}^j}{f^j}\right) + \sum \frac{a^j(w)^j}{W}\left(\frac{\dot{w}^{sj}}{w^{sj}}\right). \tag{6.2}$$

The first two sets of terms are nuisance variables. The last set of terms contains the variables of interest. The influence of overtime was accounted for by prior adjustment to the underlying quarterly average hourly earning series, but the first set of nuisance variables, representing interindustry shifts, was added to the list of explanatory variables.

If three-digit industries are considered to be "plants," each $\dot{a}^j$ may be represented by the change from the preceding period to the current period of the share of production worker man hours of the three-digit industry in total production worker man hours of the two-digit industry. Since $\sum \dot{a}^j = 0$, one cannot estimate an equation with all the $\dot{a}^j$ on the right-hand side. In fact, the Bureau of Labor Statistics has not published data from which one could construct an exhaustive set of weights for any industry. In each two-digit industry there is always a residual sector that may be highly nonhomogeneous for which detailed statistics have not been published. Therefore, as many three-digit $\dot{a}^j$ as existed for which data were published were added to the right-hand side of the basic two-digit industry equations.

Man-hour weight change variables were constructed for the following three-digit industries:

Two-Digit Code	Associated Three-Digit Codes
Durable Industries	
32	324
	325
	326
33	331
	332
	336
34	341
	342
	344
35	354
	355
36	361
Nondurable Industries	
26	265
28	283
	287–1, 2
30	301

6.3.
Construction of Overtime Series for Missing Years

The aggregation problem involved in accounting for the effects of changes in overtime was ignored, and corrections were based on an overtime factor $F = 1 + 0.5[(H - H^s)^+/H]$ for each two-digit industry. In order to calculate F it was first necessary to construct overtime series for the years before 1956. The two-digit series for average overtime hours published by the Bureau of Labor Statistics begin in January, 1956. Quarterly overtime series for each industry of this study were constructed from 1947 through 1955. An equation relating production workers' average weekly overtime hours to production workers' average weekly hours was estimated using quarterly averages of monthly data published by the Bureau of Labor Statistics. The period of fit was the second quarter of 1956 through the second quarter of 1966 (1956.2 through 1966.2). The coefficients of that equation and published series on weekly hours (which begin in 1947 or earlier for every two-digit industry) were used to extrapolate overtime hours backwards.

The relationship of average overtime hours, as defined by the Bureau of Labor Statistics, to average total hours depends on the distribution of hours worked per week in different plants in the industry. The Bureau's figure is the average of positive overtime hours. Negative overtime—the difference between hours paid for and the standard workweek when hours paid for are less than the standard workweek—is not counted.

Let $f(h)$ be the density function (percentage of all production workers) of total hours worked per week in the industry. (The j superscript is now dropped in favor of a continuous representation of firms.) The average algebraic excess of total hours over standard hours is (since standard hours have been assumed to be uniform throughout each industry):

$$(H - H^s) = \int_0^\infty (h - H^s) f(h) \, dh$$
$$= \int_0^\infty h f(h) \, dh - H^s$$
$$= H - H^s.$$

Construction of Overtime Series for Missing Years

But $(H - H^s)^+$, as defined by the Bureau, is

$$(H - H^s) = \int_{H^s}^{\infty} (h - H^s) f(h) \, dh. \tag{6.3}$$

It is not clear from the definition of H in the Bureau of Labor Statistics Bulletin 1312–14, p. 782, whether

$$(H - H^s)^+ = \int_{H^s}^{\infty} (h - H^s) f(h) \, dh,$$

or

$$(H - H^s)^+ = \frac{\int_{H^s}^{\infty} (h - H^s) f(h) \, dh}{\int_{H^s}^{\infty} f(h) \, dh}.$$

Mr. Edward T. O'Donnell, assistant regional director for manpower and employment statistics in Boston, informed the author that the definition is the first of these two. The Bureau collects from each firm in the sample the total number of hours that were paid for at overtime rates and the total number of production workers on the payroll but not the number of production workers receiving overtime pay.

If one specifies the form of $f(h)$, one can derive a prediction equation from Eq. 6.3. For algebraic simplicity it was assumed that $f(h)$ is a rectangular distribution with mean H and range δ. Equation 6.3 becomes

$$(H - H^s)^+ = \int_{H^s}^{H^s + (\delta/2)} \frac{(h - H^s)}{\delta} \, dh$$

$$= \frac{1}{2\delta} \left[H^2 - 2\left(H^s - \frac{\delta}{2}\right) H + \left(H^s - \frac{\delta}{2}\right)^2 \right], \tag{6.4}$$

which is of the form

$$(H - H^s)^+ = a - bH + cH^2; \qquad a, b, c > 0. \tag{6.5}$$

Three seasonal dummy variables representing changes in overtime due to seasonal changes in the employment weights of sectors within each two-digit industry were included in our estimates of

Table 6.2. Quarterly Overtime Equations (1956.2 through 1966.2; 41 observations) Dependent Variable: Average Weekly Overtime Hours of Production Workers

	S.I.C.* 32	S.I.C. 33	S.I.C. 34	S.I.C. 35	S.I.C. 36	S.I.C. 26	S.I.C. 28	S.I.C. 30
R^2	0.958	0.942	0.969	0.988	0.927	0.960	0.952	0.896
S.E.E.†	0.134	0.212	0.126	0.114	0.155	0.103	0.091	0.295
D-W†	1.32	0.95	1.60	1.59	1.29	1.70	1.85	0.39
H	−7.27 (−3.638)	−5.07 (−4.34)	−11.01 (−5.143)	−6.73 (−6.836)	−11.51 (−2.428)	−16.15 (−4.669)	−22.41 (−3.819)	−11.89 (−4.298)
H^2	0.0979 (4.009)	0.0703 (4.816)	0.1449 (5.544)	0.0914 (7.743)	0.1543 (2.620)	0.2008 (4.927)	0.2819 (3.972)	0.1573 (4.591)
Constant	137.0 (3.352)	92.3 (3.955)	210.8 (4.807)	124.9 (6.086)	215.3 (2.257)	327.9 (4.469)	447.2 (3.686)	226.1 (4.050)

The t statistic is recorded in parentheses under each parameter.
*The names of the Standard Industrial Classification industries are listed in Table 6.1.
†S.E.E. and D-W stand for the standard error of estimate and the Durbin–Watson statistic, respectively. These abbreviations are used in all subsequent tables of results.

Eq. 6.5. These estimates are presented in Table 6.2. The standard error is less than 0.15 hour in five out of eight cases. The critical value of the t statistic for a one-tailed test at the 0.05 level is 1.69. In all eight industries the coefficients of both H and H^2 pass this test.

One can calculate from the coefficients, the implied estimates $\hat{\delta}$ and $\hat{H}^s$. Two values can be calculated for $\hat{H}^s$, one using the constant term, the other the coefficient of H. Let them be $\hat{H}^s(a)$ and $\hat{H}^s(b)$. How close these two estimates are to being equal is a good test of the model. In fact, $\hat{H}^s(a)$ and $\hat{H}^s(b)$ were very close. In all cases the difference between them was less than 1 percent. Values of $\hat{H}^s(a)$ and $\hat{\delta}$ are presented in Tables 6.3 and 6.4. The estimates of both the standard workweek and the range of H appear reasonable.

6.4.
Importance of Compositional and Seasonal Effects

The overtime series whose construction is derived in Section 6.3 were used to calculate overtime factors for each industry which were in turn used to adjust average hourly earnings to remove the influence of changes in overtime:

$$W^s = \frac{W}{F}.$$

The rate of change (more precisely the first difference of the logarithm) of the resulting series for earnings excluding overtime were then regressed on the $\dot{a}^j$ (Δa^j in discrete time) terms discussed above plus three seasonal dummy variables, I, II, and III. The seasonal dummies were primarily intended to account for seasonal composition effects not captured by the Δa^j terms.

Table 6.3. Estimates of the Standard Workweek, in Hours* (arranged in descending order)

S.I.C.	Industry Name	$\hat{H}^s(a)$
26	Paper and allied products	41.7
28	Chemicals and allied products	40.7
32	Stone, clay, and glass products	40.0
33	Primary metal industries	39.9
34	Fabricated metal products	39.9
35	Machinery	39.8
30	Rubber and miscellaneous plastic products	39.5
36	Electrical equipment and supplies	39.2

*The figures are for $\hat{H}^s(a)$, one of the two possible estimates.

Table 6.4. Estimates of the Range of the Distribution of Weekly Hours of Production Workers, δ (arranged in descending order)

S.I.C.	Industry Name	$\hat{\delta}$
33	Primary metal industries	7.3
35	Machinery	5.5
32	Stone, clay, and glass products	5.1
36	Electrical equipment and supplies	3.6
34	Fabricated metal products	3.5
30	Rubber and miscellaneous plastic products	3.2
26	Paper and allied products	2.5
28	Chemicals and allied products	1.8

The results that are reported in Table 6.5 provide a preliminary measure of the importance of variations in earnings, excluding overtime, which are due to compositional and seasonal variables. The high percentage of variation explained by these variables in some industries should be kept in mind in judging the industry wage results presented in the next chapter. The coefficient of

Table 6.5. Man-hour Weight Changes, Seasonal Variables (1954.1 through 1969.2; 62 observations) Dependent Variable: Change in the Logarithm of Average Hourly Earnings of Production Workers Excluding Overtime.

	S.I.C. 32	S.I.C. 33*	S.I.C. 34	S.I.C. 35	S.I.C. 36	S.I.C. 26	S.I.C. 28	S.I.C. 30
R^2	0.0913	0.6254	0.2381	0.2600	0.3187	0.2956	0.5651	0.5826
S.E.E.	0.0059	0.0086	0.0053	0.0043	0.0065	0.0038	0.0047	0.0060
D-W	1.66	1.79	1.52	0.944	1.53	1.05	1.51	1.66
Δa^1	−0.271 (−1.03)	0.394 (2.22)	0.0755 (0.318)	0.0051 (0.042)	0.0974 (1.71)	−0.152 (−0.942)	0.099 (0.311)	0.425 (6.88)
Δa^2	−0.447 (−1.79)	0.1964 (0.497)	−0.0446 (−0.142)	−0.0074 (−0.023)			−0.801 (−3.45)	
Δa^3	−0.228 (−0.68)	0.1643 (0.1964)	0.0431 (0.322)					
Constant	0.0101 (4.11)	0.012 (4.37)	0.0123 (4.35)	0.0128 (11.35)	0.0120 (7.11)	0.0089 (6.38)	0.0094 (6.23)	0.0144 (9.09)
I	−0.0023 (−0.967)	−0.0037 (−0.957)	0.0002 (0.0502)	−0.0028 (−1.49)	0.0005 (0.194)	−0.0007 (−0.256)	0.0040 (1.92)	−0.0084 (−3.87)
II	−0.0016 (−0.349)	−0.0070 (−1.7)	−0.0052 (−1.19)	−0.0049 (−3.01)	−0.0048 (−2.05)	0.0003 (0.215)	0.0048 (2.22)	−0.0100 (−4.62)
III	−0.0017 (−0.478)	0.0025 (0.704)	−0.0080 (−1.94)	−0.0065 (−3.93)	−0.0090 (−3.83)	0.0057 (3.92)	−0.0076 (−1.33)	−0.0033 (−1.47)

The t statistic is recorded in parentheses beneath each coefficient.
*Two dummy variables for strikes in 1956.3 and 1959.3, 4 were also included. Their coefficients and t statistics are

0.0119 (1.3)
−0.0168 (−2.5)

multiple correlation, R^2, runs from 0.09 (S.I.C. 32) to 0.625 (S.I.C. 33).[1] It is greater than 0.5 in three cases.

6.5.
Estimation of Long-Run Value Productivity

The term PX/E was constructed as the product of P, an industry output price index, and X/E, long-run average labor productivity. Unfortunately, the commodity classification on which the Bureau of Labor Statistics publishes its wholesale price indices does not agree with the Standard Industrial Classification, on which it publishes earnings, hours, and employment data. However, Eckstein and Wyss [1970] have constructed quarterly output price indices for two-digit industries in manufacturing by recombining finely disaggregated commodity codes taking account of secondary product shipments. The parameter P was represented by their index for each industry.

Since long-run labor productivity cannot be observed directly, it must be calculated from estimates of a model of the cyclical behavior of productivity. The model used was a modified version of what has come to be known as Okun's law.[2] A simple relationship between current output and current inputs was postulated according to which the elasticity of output to inputs can be greater than or less than one. It turned out that all the estimates of the short-run elasticity of output to man hours were close to unity.

The equation that was estimated is a highly simplified version of an equation described by Modigliani [1968] and Sutch [1967]. It re-

1. It is important that R^2 is not adjusted for degrees of freedom and that it reflects the explanatory power of the constant term as well as that of the nuisance variables.
2. Okun's law relates percentage changes in GNP to percentage point changes in the unemployment rate, roughly in the ratio of 3 to 1. See Okun [1962].

lates current man hours not to current output but to capacity output. This slightly unusual relationship is developed from two other, more intuitive, relationships. The first is an equation stating that the ratio of current man hours to man hours at full capacity is a function of the utilization rate. This is the equation that resembles Okun's law. The second is an equation stating that labor productivity at full capacity grows at varying trend rates. A special procedure for estimating kinked time trends was used.

The first equation was

$$\frac{M}{M^*} = e^{-\mu(X^*-X)/X^*}, \tag{6.6}$$

where M^* is the man hours of production workers required to produce capacity output X^*. Let M^* be called full-capacity man hours. The fraction of full-capacity man hours required to produce any given output X varies with the implied rate of excess capacity $(X^* - X)/X^*$. Note that

$$X = X^* \leftrightarrow M = M^*,$$

$$X = 0 \leftrightarrow \frac{M}{M^*} = e^{-\mu}.$$

Since $e^{-\mu}$ is the ratio of overhead man hours to full-capacity man hours, there will be a nonzero amount of overhead labor.[3] Accordingly, the elasticity of output with respect to production–worker man hours varies with the inverse of the utilization rate. That elasticity is $(1/\mu)(X^*/X)$.

---

3. If μ were equal to unity, which would imply unitary elasticity of output with respect to man-hours at full capacity, the ratio of overhead man hours to total man-hours would be approximately 0.37.

The second equation was

$$\frac{X^*}{M^*} = \eta e^{\Sigma_i r_i \tau_i}. \tag{6.7}$$

Labor productivity at full capacity grows at varying exponential rates. The construction of the τ_i variables will be explained shortly. It was such as to permit the growth path of productivity to have kinks.

The equation that was actually estimated was obtained by solving for M^* in Eq. 6.7 and substituting that expression into Eq. 6.6. The result is an equation in which the ratio of capacity output to current man hours is a function of the utilization rate and different time trends.

$$\frac{X^*}{M} = \eta e^{\Sigma_i r_i \tau_i} e^{\mu[(X^* - X)/X^*]}.$$

Taking natural logarithms of both sides and lagging the excess capacity measure over two quarters in order to capture dynamic effects, one obtains

$$\log \left(\frac{X^*}{M}\right)_t = \log \eta + \sum r_i \tau_{it} + \mu_1 \left(\frac{X^* - X}{X^*}\right)_t + \mu_2$$
$$\times \left(\frac{X^* - X}{X^*}\right)_{t-1}; \quad \mu_1 + \mu_2 = \mu \tag{6.8}$$

This equation was estimated from quarterly data for the period 1948.2 through 1968.4. For all industries except Fabricated Metal Products (S.I.C. 34), an unpublished Federal Reserve Board index of capacity utilization by industry was used to represent X/X^*.[4]

---
4. The construction of the Federal Reserve Board index for manufacturing, the only index currently published, is discussed in de Leeuw [1966] and Enzler [1967].

The Federal Reserve Board index was not available for S.I.C. 34, and therefore the revised Wharton School utilization index was used for that industry.[5] For all industries, X was represented by the Federal Reserve Board index of production, quarterly, seasonally adjusted; M was man hours of production workers scaled so that the 1958 average of each series was 1.0.

The linked time-trend variables were constructed in the following manner: Let t represent time in quarters, with 1947.1 arbitrarily set equal to unity. Let the ith time trend begin in quarter n_i. Then the ith time trend was defined as

$\tau_i = 0 \qquad\quad t = 1, n_i - 1$

$\tau_i = t - n_i + 1 \quad t = n_i, n_{i+1} - 1$

$\tau_i = n_{i+1} - n_i \quad t = n_{i+1}, 88$

Figure 6.1 depicts two such trends, τ_1 and τ_2, the first beginning in 1947.1 and the second in the kth quarter. The estimate of the trend for the whole period is the sum of the products of the individual τ_i's and their coefficients.

The choice of the number of trends and their breaking points was based on the behavior of the capacity utilization indices. To summarize briefly, the trend rate of growth was assumed to be constant between quarters of peak capacity utilization that were spaced at least three years apart. This procedure resulted in most cases in breaking points near the end of 1950, of 1955, of 1959, and of 1966, implying thus five periods of constant rate of growth.

Since the man hours index in the denominator of the productivity term was not seasonally adjusted, dummy variables equal to one

5. The Wharton indices, which are based on estimates of capacity constructed by linking peaks in output, were revised by Klein and Preston [1967], on the basis of industry production function studies. The revised indices appear in Klein and Summers [1966] and were updated with data kindly supplied by the Economics Research Unit, University of Pennsylvania.

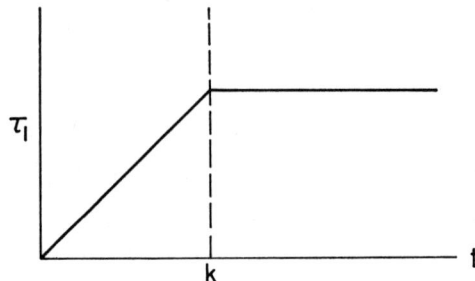

a. Trend τ_1 Rises in First Period, then Levels off.

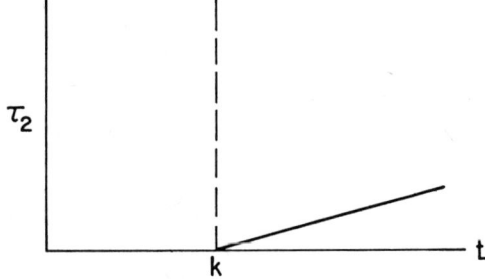

b. Trend τ_2 Is Zero in First Period, Rises in Second.

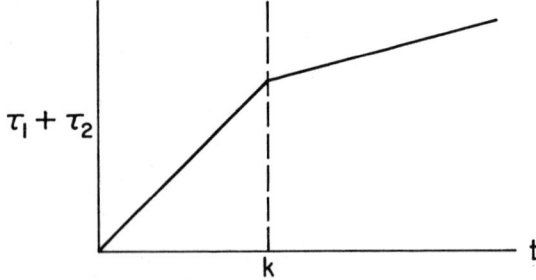

c. Trend for the Whole Period = $\tau_1 + \tau_2$.

Figure 6.1. Construction of Broken Time Trends

Estimation of Long-Run Value Productivity

Table 6.6. Productivity Equations (1948.2 through 1968.4; 83 observations)
Dependent Variable: Logarithm of the Ratio of Capacity to Man Hours

	S.I.C. 32	S.I.C. 33*	S.I.C. 34	S.I.C. 35	S.I.C. 36	S.I.C. 26	S.I.C. 28	S.I.C. 30
R^2	0.9946	0.9895	0.9941	0.9898	0.9835	0.9963	0.9989	0.9796
S.E.E.	0.0198	0.0256	0.0203	0.0206	0.0360	0.0144	0.0148	0.0277
D-W	1.6459	1.1951	1.1754	0.4971	0.5539	0.7917	1.190	0.7898
$[(X^* - X)/X^*]_t$	0.8462 (9.62)	0.9141 (23.1)	1.0772 (13.5)	1.2127 (35.9)	0.5380 (5.0)	0.4356 (6.9)	0.2180 (2.31)	0.7014 (9.19)
$[(X^* - X)/X^*]_{t-1}$	0.2041 (2.36)	0.1634 (4.3)	0.1455 (1.9)		0.6350 (6.2)	0.2300 (3.7)	0.5860 (6.51)	0.4047 (5.41)
τ_1	0.0126 (8.9)	0.0042 (2.5)	0.0042 (3.1)	0.0091 (8.6)	0.0097 (2.9)	0.0067 (7.8)	0.0228 (21.2)	0.0052 (2.24)
τ_2	0.0057 (9.2)	0.0063 (9.1)	0.0050 (7.5)	0.0039 (5.8)	0.0110 (12.6)	0.0086 (19.3)	0.0159 (31.9)	0.0091 (10.8)
τ_3	0.0100 (13.1)	0.0068 (6.4)	0.0094 (11.0)	0.0106 (12.8)	0.0065 (4.8)	0.0092 (18.1)	0.0205 (40.2)	0.0117 (15.2)
τ_4	0.0067 (17.0)	0.0063 (9.2)	0.0083 (19.6)	0.0073 (23.5)	0.0081 (10.0)	0.0084 (29.2)	0.0158 (33.7)	0.0080 (15.0)
τ_5	0.0077 (6.3)	0.0015 (0.83)	0.0027 (1.9)		0.0016 (0.51)	0.0074 (7.2)	0.0134 (28.3)	0.0069 (2.8)
Constant	−0.7396 (−34.1)	−0.5838 (−23.8)	−0.6033 (−30.7)	−0.8127 (−38.6)	−0.8142 (−17.9)	−0.50 (−38.8)	−1.11 (−58.8)	−0.6644 (−16.9)

The t statistic is recorded in parentheses under each parameter.
*Three dummy variables were added for strikes in 1952.2, 3, 1956.3, and 1959.3, 4. Their coefficients and t statistics are
−0.0203 (−1.00)
−0.0440 (−1.58)
−0.0109 (−0.53)

in the first, second, and third quarters were added to the right-hand side of Eq. 6.8.

Results are presented in Table 6.6. High values of the squared correlation coefficients notwithstanding, the equations leave much of the short-run movements of productivity unexplained. The standard errors are large and the Durbin–Watson statics low. Nevertheless, the μ coefficients are highly significant in all industries. From these coefficients one can calculate, for any given level of capacity utilization, the implied elasticity of output to man hours. The estimated values of these elasticities at full capacity are presented in Table 6.7.

The purpose behind Eq. 6.8 was to estimate the growth rates r_i.

These estimates, which are summarized in Table 6.8, warrant several general comments: (1) There is mild evidence of exceptionally high rates of growth which may reflect reorganization of production, renewal of equipment, and elimination of numerous bottlenecks in the period right after World War II. In four out of eight industries this is the period with either the highest or second-

Table 6.7. Short-run Elasticity of Output with Respect to Production Worker Man-hours at Full Capacity* (arranged in descending order)

S.I.C.	Industry Name	Elasticity
26	Paper and allied products	1.5124
28	Chemicals and allied products	1.2438
32	Stone, clay, and glass products	0.9521
33	Primary metal industries	0.9281
30	Rubber and miscellaneous plastic products	0.9041
36	Electrical equipment and supplies	0.8528
35	Machinery	0.8246
34	Fabricated metal products	0.8179

*Elasticity at capacity = $(\hat{\mu} X^*/X^*)^{-1} = \hat{\mu}^{-1}$, where $\hat{\mu} = \hat{\mu}_1 + \hat{\mu}_2$.

Table 6.8. Trend Rates of Growth and Productivity

S.I.C.	Annual Rates of Growth (percent)				
32	48.1–51.1 5.04	51.2–55.4 2.28	56.1–59.3 4.00	59.4–66.1 2.68	66.2–68.4 3.08
33	48.1–51.1 1.68	51.2–56.2 2.52	56.3–60.1 2.72	60.2–66.2 2.52	66.3–68.4 0.60
34	48.1–50.3 1.68	50.4–55.3 2.00	55.4–59.2 3.76	59.3–66.2 3.32	66.3–68.4 1.08
35	48.1–52.1 3.64	52.2–56.3 1.56	56.4–59.3 4.24	59.4–68.4 2.92*	
36	48.1–50.3 3.88	50.4–56.2 4.40	56.3–60.1 2.60	60.2–66.3 3.24	66.4–68.4 0.64
26	48.1–51.2 2.68	51.3–55.4 3.44	56.1–59.3 3.68	59.4–66.2 3.36	66.3–68.4 2.96
28	48.1–51.1 9.12	51.2–55.4 6.36	56.1–59.3 8.20	59.4–63.4 6.32	64.1–68.4 5.36
30	48.1–50.4 2.08	51.1–55.2 3.64	55.3–59.3 4.68	59.4–66.4 3.20	67.1–68.4 2.76

*An initial estimate of negative rate of growth for 1967.1 through 1968.4 was rejected and the final two periods were combined to produce the result stated.

highest rate of growth. (2) Trend rates of growth appear to have been particularly high between the cyclical peaks of 1955–56 and 1959. These results support the views that the general weakness of actual productivity (as opposed to trend productivity) in that period was related to the weakness of the 1959 expansion and that technologically the period benefited from the capital boom of 1955–1956. (3) Estimated trend rates of growth decline markedly after 1966, a result that may be due to diminishing returns at very high rates of capacity utilization. It is noticeable that in six out of eight cases the post-1966 estimated rate of growth is lower than the 1951–1955 rate. Though diminishing returns of this sort are a cyclical phenomenon, it is very different from the type of cyclical labor hoarding that is known to influence markedly any actual labor productivity during periods of low utilization, and it is likely that it would have as great an influence on wage negotiations as would noncyclical technological developments. Therefore, it seems appropriate to keep the post-1966 slowdown in full-capacity productivity implied by these estimates in the wage equations of the next chapter. (4) Across industries there is a substantial variation in rates of growth, going from the high figures of the relatively new Chemicals and Allied Products industry to the lows of the sluggish Primary Metal industry.

The productivity variable used in subsequent wage equations is log $[P(X/E)]$. It was calculated in the following manner:

$$\log P \frac{X}{E^t} = \log P_t + \log \hat{\eta} + \sum \hat{r}_i \tau_{it},$$

where P_t is the value of Eckstein–Wyss industry output price index in the tth quarter. The variable τ_{it} is the value of the ith trend variable in the tth quarter. The parameters $\log \hat{\eta}$ and $\hat{r}_i$ were estimated in the productivity equations.

6.6.
Nonunion Wages and Turnover Rates

The series on average compensation per man hour in trade, services, and government enterprises which was used to represent W^a in Eq. 5.6 was adjusted in several ways. First, it was constructed as a fixed-weight average, holding the weights of the three industry groups constant at their 1958 averages. Second, the effect on total compensation of changes in overtime on the one hand, and both social security and unemployment tax rates on the other, were removed with the help of estimates of the effects of these variables taken from an unpublished study by the author in which the rate of change of compensation per man hour in these sectors was regressed on the change in a measure of overtime and in the tax rates plus other variables. The estimated coefficients obtained there were used here to subtract the effects of these variables from the observed rate of change of compensation per man hour, and the resulting computed rate of change excluding these factors was cumulated to obtain an index of compensation per man hour with these effects removed. That index was rebased on the actual value of compensation per man hour in the chosen sectors in 1950.1. Then W_t^a was represented by the value of the rebased index in the tth quarter.

Continuous quarterly series for layoffs, the turnover rate used to represent N_t in Eq. 5.6, were constructed from two-digit industry series on a 1957 Standard Industrial Classification basis from January 1958 through June 1969, published by the Bureau of Labor Statistics in *Employment and Earnings in the United States, 1909–69*, and two-digit industry series on a 1947 Standard Industrial Classification basis from January 1950 through October 1961, published in the *Monthly Labor Review*. Definitions differ for the two sets of series. The size of the Bureau of Labor Statistics sample was also different for the two sets.

The 1947 and 1957 S.I.C. series were linked in the following manner: Let N' = a 1957 S.I.C. series, and N = a 1947 S.I.C. series. It was assumed that

$$N' = AN^\gamma e^{rt},$$

$$\log N' = \log A + \gamma \log N + rt. \tag{6.9}$$

This is a slight generalization of the common assumption that the ratio of a 1957 S.I.C. series to its 1947 S.I.C. counterpart is constant.

Equation 6.9 allows for divergent trends in the two series, reflecting the increasing or diminishing importance of sectors included in one series and omitted in the other. It was estimated with quarterly data from 1958.1 through 1961.2, the period of overlap between the two sets of series. Quarterly rates were constructed by cumulating monthly rates. Three seasonal variables were added to the right-hand side to allow for seasonal changes in the relative importance of sectors included in one and excluded in the other series. When the coefficient of the time trend did not pass a two-tailed test for significance at the 0.05 level, we reestimated the equation without the time trend. Coefficients of the final form of the equation were used along with the 1947 S.I.C. series to extrapolate backwards a 1957 S.I.C. series for each turnover rate and each industry. The constructed series run from 1950.1 through 1957.4, at which time they join the currently published series. The extrapolated-plus-current series from 1950.1 through 1966.2 were seasonally adjusted using a ratio-to-moving average program. Finally, if we let N represent henceforth this constructed series, N_{t-1} in Eq. 5.6 was replaced by the two-quarter moving average,

$$0.5 \ (N_{t-1} + N_{t-2}),$$

in order to allow for a more lagged response.

In Eq. 5.6 the layoff rate itself is entered, not its logarithm. This is primarily because layoffs are not trend dominated. However, one can also interpret N as the logarithm of a labor force over employment ratio.

The layoff rate was entered as a decimal. Since it is of the order of magnitude of 0.01, $N \sim \log(1 + N)$. The term $(1 + N)$ = the ratio of current employees plus recently layed-off employees to current employees. This ratio bears some resemblance to the labor force over employment ratio.

6.7.
Summary

Data series have now been constructed for each variable in Eq. 5.6.

1. Some of the movements of average hourly earnings reflecting influences other than movements of wage rates have been accounted for. This has been done by adjusting earnings for overtime and by constructing variables that measure changes in the share of man hours of labor in low-wage and high-wage sectors. Changes in earnings due to changes in the average quality of the work force are still unaccounted for.

2. Separate indices were obtained for the price component and the real productivity component of value productivity. These were then multiplied together. The real productivity component measures real productivity at full capacity. It consists of a series of four or five linked exponential trends.

3. Average compensation per man hour in trade, services, and government enterprises, the measure chosen to represent nonunion wages, was adjusted for the effects of overtime and employment taxes in order to render it more comparable to the average hourly earnings series used for the dependent variable.

4. The layoff rate was chosen as a measure of labor-market conditions, and a continuous layoff series was constructed.

5. The only variable for which an official series was used directly as published is the cost-of-living index. The Bureau of Labor Statistics' consumer price index is $\mathscr{P}_t$ in Eq. 5.6. Again, in order to allow for a more lagged response, $\Delta \ln \mathscr{P}_{t-1}$ in Eq. 5.6 was replaced by $0.5(\ln \mathscr{P}_{t-1} - \ln \mathscr{P}_{t-3})$.

The construction of these variables involved the analysis of two problems that are otherwise somewhat separate from the main topic: the behavior of average overtime hours and the determinants of cyclical and trend movements of productivity. Findings relative to these two problems were the following:

1. It was possible to derive, from the assumption that the intraindustry density function of production worker hours is uniform, an equation relating overtime hours to total hours for which reasonable estimates were obtained. This suggests that either the density function is approximately uniform or the relationship estimated is insensitive to the particular form of that density function.

2. The important findings concerning real productivity relate to its trend. Wide variations were found in estimates of the trend rate of growth of productivity in different industries, and within a given industry in different periods. Large trend rates of increase of productivity were observed in most industries between 1955–56 and 1959 and in some in the period between 1948 and the Korean War. Marked deceleration was found in many industries after 1966. All of these variations were considered to be relevant factors liable to influence wage change in the context of the bargaining equation to be estimated in the next chapter.

7

Estimation Results

7.1.
Introduction

Inspection of Eq. 5.6, particularly the version with the additional one-quarter lag that was actually estimated, reveals close similarity to the Phillips [1958] curve.

$$\Delta \ln W_t = d_0 + \lambda d_1 \ln \left(\frac{PX}{E}\right)_{t-1} + \lambda d_2 \ln W_{t-1}^a$$

$$+ 0.5\lambda d_3 (N_{t-1} + N_{t-2}) - \lambda \ln W_{t-1}$$

$$+ 0.5 d_4 (\ln \mathscr{P}_{t-1} - \ln \mathscr{P}_{t-3}) + d_5 G_t. \qquad (5.6')$$

In fact, if the terms in $(PX/E)_{t-1}$, W_{t-1}^a, and W_{t-1} are removed from the right-hand side, what remains is a Phillips curve in which the inverse of the unemployment rate has been replaced by the layoff rate. Consequently, it is the estimates of the coefficients of these three variables which are crucial from the point of view of the bargaining theory to be tested. The appropriate null hypothesis is not that all the coefficients of Eq. 5.6' are zero but that the bargaining variables $(PX/E)_{t-1}$, W_{t-1}^a, and W_{t-1} do not add significantly to the explanatory power of the equation. In this chapter's presentation of eight least-squares estimates of Eq. 5.6', emphasis will be placed on the sign, significance, and magnitude of the coefficients of these three variables.

7.2.
Industry Phillips Curves

A good point of departure is the estimation of the quasi-Phillips curves obtained by dropping the bargaining variables from Eq. 5.6'.

Table 7.1. Phillips Curves with Layoff Rates (1954.1 through 1969.2; 62 observations)
Dependent Variable: Quarterly Rate of Change of Average Hourly Earnings Excluding Overtime

	S.I.C. 32	S.I.C.* 33	S.I.C. 34	S.I.C. 35	S.I.C. 36	S.I.C. 26	S.I.C. 28	S.I.C. 30
R^2	0.3250	0.7025	0.4756	0.5885	0.4831	0.5578	0.6812	0.6447
S.E.E.	0.0052	0.0079	0.0045	0.0033	0.0058	0.0031	0.0041	0.0057
D-W	2.2795	2.0561	2.0901	1.8143	1.9912	1.7327	1.9179	1.9988
$0.5(N_{t-1} + N_{t-2})$	−0.1519 (−3.1)	0.0043 (0.10)	−0.0343 (−1.1)	−0.0624 (−2.5)	−0.1157 (−2.0)	−0.1898 (−3.4)	−0.1320 (−1.6)	−0.0404 (−0.79)
$0.5(\log \mathscr{P}_{t-1} - \log \mathscr{P}_{t-3})$	0.2462 (1.3)	0.5326 (1.7)	0.4540 (2.4)	0.4126 (3.2)	0.2627 (1.1)	0.1562 (1.3)	0.0359 (0.22)	0.2030 (0.93)
G_t	−0.0025 (−1.7)	−0.0068 (−2.8)	−0.0041 (−3.0)	−0.0041 (−4.1)	−0.0053 (−3.1)	−0.0028 (−3.2)	−0.0048 (−4.1)	−0.0041 (−2.5)
Constant	0.0180 (4.7)	0.0108 (3.0)	0.0116 (3.0)	0.0139 (8.1)	0.0162 (4.6)	0.0134 (6.3)	0.0133 (4.8)	0.0162 (4.7)

The t statistic is recorded in parentheses under each parameter.
Included with the variables listed on the right-hand side of the estimated equation were the compositional and seasonal variables discussed in Section 6.4.

*Dummy variables were included for strikes in 1956.3 and 1959.3, 4. Their coefficients and t statistics are
0.0082   (1.0)
−0.0199 (−3.1)

The results, which are presented in Table 7.1, are unimpressive. The percentage of variance explained is high for quarterly wage equations, but it must be remembered that much of this reflects the explanatory power of compositional and seasonal variables (see Section 6.4). The layoff rate is significant at the 10-percent level in five out of eight cases, but the change in the cost of living in only three out of eight cases. Somewhat surprisingly the guidepost dummy is significant in all cases and, after the constant term, is the most significant variable in six cases.

7.3.
Bargaining Equations

The consequences of adding the three bargaining variables, and hence the success of this study's wage equation and of the model underlying it, may be evaluated by examining Table 7.2. Discussion of these results can be divided into discussion of the estimated coefficients of the bargaining variables and of the effect of these variables on the other parameter estimates in the equation.

In seven out of eight cases the coefficients of all three of these bargaining variables have the correct sign. The only exception is S.I.C. 35, Nonelectrical Machinery, in which the productivity variable has the wrong sign. Statistically, the null hypothesis that the addition of these three variables does not reduce unexplained variance is rejected at the 10-percent level in seven out of eight cases. The exception this time is S.I.C. 36, Electrical Equipment and Supplies.

The test statistic for this hypothesis is an F statistic equal to the ratio of the reduction in sum of squared residuals between Tables 7.1 and 7.2 to the remaining sum of squared residuals in Table 7.2, each sum being corrected for degrees of

Table 7.2. Productivity and Wages (1954.1 through 1969.2, 62 observations)
Dependent Variable: Quarterly Rate of Change of Average Hourly Earnings Excluding Overtime

	S.I.C. 32	S.I.C. 33*	S.I.C. 34	S.I.C. 35	S.I.C. 36	S.I.C. 26	S.I.C. 28	S.I.C. 30
R^2	0.4628	0.7371	0.5602	0.6440	0.5277	0.6605	0.7230	0.7016
S.E.E.	0.0048	0.0077	0.0042	0.0031	0.0057	0.0028	0.0039	0.0054
D-W	1.8587	2.0561	2.1250	1.9146	1.8782	1.6282	2.1012	1.9084
$\log [P(X/E)]_{t-1}$	0.1466 (3.2)	0.0588 (1.2)	0.0347 (1.1)	0.0135 (−0.62)	0.0654 (1.6)	0.0907 (3.1)	0.0179 (0.50)	0.0647 (2.0)
$\log W^a_{t-1}$	0.0909 (2.4)	0.0039 (0.15)	0.0500 (1.7)	0.0521 (1.8)	0.0646 (1.8)	0.0794 (2.5)	0.0129 (0.46)	0.0583 (2.3)
$\log W_{t-1}$	−0.3235 (−3.4)	−0.0946 (−1.6)	−0.1212 (−2.3)	−0.0560 (−1.1)	−0.1558 (−2.1)	−0.2034 (−3.4)	−0.0610 (−1.1)	−0.1920 (−2.8)
$0.5(N_{t-1} + N_{t-2})$	−0.1727 (−2.9)	0.0308 (0.62)	0.0084 (0.19)	−0.0346 (−1.1)	−0.0525 (−0.68)	−0.1085 (−1.4)	−0.2350 (−2.1)	−0.0092 (−0.16)
$0.5(\log \mathscr{P}_{t-1} - \log \mathscr{P}_{t-3})$	0.4576 (1.9)	0.9229 (2.2)	0.6079 (2.6)	0.5721 (3.5)	0.3158 (1.1)	0.1746 (1.2)	0.3839 (1.6)	0.2746 (0.98)
G_t	0.0005 (0.27)	−0.0035 (−1.3)	−0.0028 (−1.7)	−0.0020 (−1.6)	−0.0026 (−1.2)	−0.0002 (−0.17)	−0.0026 (−1.8)	0.0004 (0.18)
Constant	0.1367 (4.0)	0.0782 (2.0)	0.0618 (2.6)	0.0322 (1.3)	0.0596 (2.9)	0.0721 (4.4)	0.0403 (2.3)	0.1000 (3.4)

The t statistic is recorded in parentheses under each parameter.
Included with the variables listed on the right-hand side of the estimated equation were the compositional and seasonal variables discussed in Section 6.4.
*Dummy variables were included for strikes in 1956.3 and 1959.3, 4. Their coefficients and t statistics are
−0.0000 (−0.005)
−0.0199 (−3.12)

freedom. These F statistics for the eight industries, arranged in descending order, were as follows:

S.I.C.	Name of Industry	F statistic	Degrees of Freedom
26	Paper and allied products	5.10	3/51
32	Stone, clay, and glass products	4.24	3/50
30	Rubber and miscellaneous plastic products	3.24	3/51
34	Fabricated metal products	3.16	3/49
35	Machinery	2.60	3/50
28	Chemicals and allied products	2.52	3/50
33	Primary metal industries	2.04	3/47
36	Electrical equipment and supplies	1.53	3/51

The F-distribution tables indicate that all the statistics except the last are significant at the 10-percent level. This result must be qualified by the recognition of the fact that, if the residuals in Table 7.2 are serially correlated, naïve application of the F test overstates the significance of coefficients. Though most of the Durbin–Watson statistics in the table are not far from two, it is also true that the presence of a lagged, dependent variable in the equation biases all Durbin–Watson statistics toward two.

In many cases, the most stringent test of a model is the degree to which the magnitude of estimated coefficients agrees with prior expectations. By this test, the estimated coefficients of $(PX/E)_{t-1}$, W^a_{t-1}, and W_{t-1} leave a little more to be desired, though they may still be considered reasonable. As is clear from inspection of Eq. 5.1, the long-run elasticities of W to $(PX - RK)/E$ (or its proxy PX/E) and to W^a should sum to unity. Moreover, their ratio should in general be equal to

$$\frac{\xi[(PX - RK)/E]}{W^a},$$

where $\xi = 1$ in the case in which the union's utility function is linear. The individual elasticities and their sums and ratios are reported in Tables 7.3 and 7.4.

The estimates of the sums, which lie between 0.5 and 0.84, are low but not so low that their difference from unity cannot be attributed to errors in variable.

In particular, underestimates of the sums in Table 7.4 may be due to the presence of relatively greater errors in the value productivity variable and the nonunion wage variable than in the lagged wage variable. Possible sources of error in the lagged wage variable include all factors other than overtime which cause movements of earnings to differ from movements of the wage rate. Sources of error in the value productivity variable include the following: (a) the difference between $(PX - RK)/E$ and PX/E if the former is not proportional to the latter; (b) the difference between transaction prices and market prices [the Bureau of Labor Statistics indices are constructed from market prices. In oligopolistic industries,

Table 7.3. Steady-State Elasticity of Wage Rate to Value Productivity and Nonunion Wage Rate (arranged in descending order)

S.I.C.	Industry Name	Elasticity to Value Productivity
33	Primary metal industries	0.60
32	Stone, clay, and glass products	0.45
26	Paper and allied products	0.45
36	Electrical equipment and supplies	0.42
30	Rubber and miscellaneous plastic products	0.34
28	Chemicals and allied products	0.29
34	Fabricated metal products	0.29
35	Machinery	−0.24
S.I.C.	Industry Name	Elasticity to Nonunion Wage Rate
35	Machinery	0.93
36	Electrical equipment and supplies	0.41
34	Fabricated metal products	0.41
26	Paper and allied products	0.39
30	Rubber and miscellaneous plastic products	0.30
32	Stone, clay, and glass products	0.28
28	Chemicals and allied products	0.21
33	Primary metal industries	0.04

transactions prices may fluctuate more than market prices]; and (c) misspecification of short-run labor demand in Section 6.5 leading to erroneous estimates of X/E. Sources of error in W^a include false identification of the trade, services, and government enterprise sector as a source of union labor for each industry; and inadequate correction for the conceptual differences between compensation per employee man hour in these sectors and the average hourly earnings of production workers series used for the dependent variable.

Since the data do not permit the calculation of $(PX - RK)/E$, it is not possible to fix a prior expectation of the ratio of the two elasticities, even for the case in which the union's utility function

Table 7.4. Sum and Ratio of Elasticities of Wage Rate to Value Productivity and Nonunion Wage Rate (arranged in descending order)

S.I.C.	Industry Name	Sum of Elasticities
26	Paper and allied products	0.84
36	Electrical equipment and supplies	0.83
32	Stone, clay, and glass products	0.73
34	Fabricated metal products	0.70
35	Machinery	0.69
33	Primary metal industries	0.64
30	Rubber and miscellaneous plastic products	0.64
28	Chemicals and allied products	0.50

S.I.C.	Industry Name	Elasticity to Value Productivity over Elasticity to Nonunion Wage
33	Primary metal industries	14.6
32	Stone, clay, and glass products	1.6
28	Chemicals and allied parts	1.4
26	Paper and allied products	1.2
30	Rubber and miscellaneous plastic products	1.1
36	Electrical equipment and supplies	1.0
34	Fabricated metal products	0.7
35	Machinery	-0.5

is linear. However, if the firm is to remain in business, $(PX - RK/E)$ must exceed W^a; this gives their ratio a reasonable minimum bound of unity. A maximum bound is harder to justify, but two seems reasonable, because it is unlikely that the demand price for labor could remain more than twice as great as its supply price for any long period of time. In five of the eight cases the estimated ratio falls within this very rough bound.

Estimates of the mean lag, based on the estimated coefficients of W_{t-1}, are presented in Table 7.5. Excluding S.I.C. 35 and 38 (mean lags of four and five years), the range of the estimates is between one and three years and appears reasonable. Table 7.6 lists standard errors of the bargaining equation.

As for the other variables in Eq. 5.6', the addition of $(PX/E)_{t-1}$, W^a_{t-1}, and W_{t-1} markedly reduces the significance of the layoff rate and renders the guidepost dummy almost negligible but results in a sharp increase in the magnitude and significance of the cost-of-living effect. The estimated value of 0.9 for the cost-of-living effect in the Primary Metal industry is particularly striking. As was

Table 7.5. Mean Lag of Wage Rate Adjustments (arranged in descending order)

S.I.C.	Industry Name	Mean Lag in Quarters
35	Machinery	18.9
28	Chemicals and allied products	17.4
33	Primary metal industries	11.6
34	Fabricated metal products	9.3
36	Electrical equipment and supplies	7.4
30	Rubber and miscellaneous plastic products	6.2
26	Paper and allied products	5.9
32	Stone, clay, and glass products	4.1

Table 7.6. Standard Errors of Bargaining Equation Compared with Means and Standard Deviations of Dependent Variable

		Percent Annual Rate of Change		
S.I.C.		Standard Error	Mean of Dependent Variable	Standard Deviation of Dependent Variable
32	Stone, clay, and glass products	1.92	3.68	2.36
33	Primary metal industries	3.08	3.68	5.24
34	Fabricated metal products	1.68	3.68	2.28
35	Machinery	1.24	3.68	1.92
36	Electrical equipment and supplies	2.28	3.52	3.04
26	Paper and allied products	1.12	4.04	1.76
28	Chemicals and allied products	1.57	3.92	2.72
30	Rubber and miscellaneous plastic products	2.16	3.20	3.60

pointed out earlier, the role of the change in the cost-of-living variable of Eq. 5.6′ is to act as a proxy for expectations of change in all the independent variables. However, the interaction between the estimated strength of this effect and the introduction of the value productivity and nonunion wage variables suggests that the proxy may be particularly capturing the effect of expectations of change in these two variables. It is difficult to pass judgment on the reduction of significance of the guidepost dummy without any prior evidence on the effectiveness of the guideposts. However, even for a believer in the guideposts the coefficients in Table 7.1 (a reduction in the annual rate of change of 2.7 percent in the Primary Metals industry, S.I.C. 33) appear too large, and the more moderate estimates in Table 7.2 appear more reasonable. Though the layoff rate keeps the right sign in six cases, it remains significant only in two. Inspection of the data suggests that this poor showing may be a natural consequence, due to collinearity, of the increase in the estimated significance of the cost-of-living effect.

7.4.
Qualifications

Though it is fair to say that the general tenor of the results of the previous section tend to support the bargaining model of this study, it should be pointed out that as quarterly wage equations the estimates in Table 7.2 still leave much to be desired. The standard errors remain high, ranging between 57 percent (Chemicals and Allied Products) and 82 percent (Stone, Clay, and Glass Products) of the standard deviation of the dependent variable.

Another important limitation of this study is its neglect of possible simultaneous equation bias. The presence of the value productivity term in Eq. 5.6' makes it somewhat similar, ignoring lags, to an inverted version of the type of markup price equation sometimes used in studies of monopoly or oligopoly pricing. Thus if one rejected the Nash model, one could argue that the industries in this study, in which the bargaining equation does explain wage change better than the Phillips curve, are in fact industries in which prices behave as predicted by the markup hypothesis. This is a serious charge. However, the criticism could just as well be turned the other way around. It may be that past success in the estimation of markup price equations in fact reflects the influence of bargaining variables like those in Eq. 5.6' on wages. Further work in which wage and price behavior are described simultaneously is needed to solve this important problem.

7.5.
Summary

It has been pointed out that the correct null hypothesis for testing the bargaining wage Eq. 5.6' is that it does not explain wage change any better than the Phillips curve. Estimates of Eq. 5.6' presented in this chapter have been viewed in that light, and, on the basis of the sign, significance, and magnitude of the estimated coefficients for $(PX/E)_{t-1}$, W^a_{t-1}, and W_{t-1}, it may be concluded that the bargaining equation does explain wage movements better than the Phillips curve in six out of the eight test industries (all of which are highly unionized industries). In six of the test industries it was simultaneously true that the coefficients of $(PX/E)_{t-1}$, W^a_{t-1}, and W_{t-1} had the correct sign and that they were jointly significantly different from zero. It has been argued earlier that validation of the bargaining equation amounts to support for the complete bilateral monopoly model and for the applicability of Nash's fixed-threat bargaining theory to employer–union negotiations—in short, to support for the central hypothesis of this study.

8

Conclusion

The empirical support found in Chapter 7 for the bargaining wage Equation 5.6′, and thus indirectly for the Nash bilateral monopoly model from which it was derived, brings this study to a close. A brief discussion of its implications is in order.

The basic accomplishment of this study has been the successful application of game theory to an area of economic activity to which the standard market models do not apply. The essence of bilateral monopoly is the conflict between two active agents, both price setters rather than price takers. In order to analyze the resolution of that conflict, reference has been made to the theory of the bargaining problem. Successful application of this branch of game theory may bode well for the application of other branches in other areas.

It is interesting, in closing, to compare briefly this study with other studies concerning the influence of unions on wages that have not involved any construction of models of bargaining as formal as the one attempted here. Three points are particularly worthy of note:

First, the basic equation, Eq. 5.3, is an equilibrium equation. Emphasis on an equilibrium relationship contrasts with many empirical studies of the influence of unions on the rate of wage changes that have been based on the Phillips curve, i.e., on a disequilibrium mechanism.[1] These include Eckstein and Wilson [1962], Perry [1966], Pierson [1968], and many others. It resembles, however, the approaches of Kuh [1967] and Sargan [1964], who have proposed equations to explain the equilibrium level of wages

---

1. In Chapter 7 the empirical equation that was compared statistically with a Phillips curve was a modified version of Eq. 5.3 onto which a lagged adjustment mechanism had been grafted. It turned out that, after the addition of the adjustment mechanism, Eq. 5.6 resembled a Phillips curve in many of its particulars. This does not make the theoretical origin of Eq. 5.6 any less different from the origin of the Phillips curve.

in aggregates encompassing both unionized and nonunionized sectors. In their studies, as in ours, simple lagged adjustment mechanisms are grafted onto the equilibrium relationships. The present study owes much to Kuh's study in particular.[2] There is no clear a priori reason for emphasizing equilibrium relationships rather than disequilibrium mechanisms. However, given the present state of knowledge, it appears to be easier to derive interesting hypotheses about the former than about the latter.

Second, our model provides an explanation, derived from first principles, of the assertion made by some labor economists that unions are able to obtain higher wages in industries that are concentrated than in those that are not concentrated.[3] The argument always was that the unions obtain a share of the monopoly profits of the employers for their members. What was missing was a formal explanation of why and how profit-maximizing employers and utility-maximizing unions would agree to profit sharing. (It should be noted that the explanation that comes out of the Nash model does not rely on non-profit-maximizing behavior by the employer.)

Because it explains what might be called profit-sharing unionism, our model is not applicable to all unionized industries: It does not explain how unions raise wages in industries in which the employers are perfect competitors. More generally, it does not explain how unions raise wages in industries in which they restrict the supply of labor by their own means. One subject of further study should be the derivation of wage equations for industries such as these.

2. This study also resembles that of Rapping [1967], which is a cross-section analysis of wage levels in highly unionized and highly concentrated industries. Rapping relates average hourly earnings in two-digit industries to—among other variables—value added per man hour or profits per man-hour.
3. See the discussion of this argument in Rees [1962], Chapter 4, Section 5.

Third, our equation relates the wage in a unionized industry to nonunion wages; this is a new twist in empirical studies of wage determination by unions. Two of the three independent variables in Eq. 5.3, value productivity and an index of cyclical conditions, have appeared—or a variant of each has appeared—in almost all empirical wage equations for industries with sizable unionized segments. Cyclical conditions are usually represented by the unemployment rate. Eckstein and Wilson [1962] and Perry [1966] and many others have included profits, which are closely related to value productivity,[4] in their wage equations. In the Kuh [1967] and Sargan [1964] studies, value productivity appears directly. But the nonunion wage is a variable that does not appear in any of these studies. The theoretical point that union wage levels cannot be understood independently of nonunion wage levels has been made by Rosen [1969] and by Ashenfelter, Johnson, and Pencavel [1971]. But no empirical estimates of the direct effect of nonunion wages on union wages has previously been made. The only empirical equations in which union wages have been related to nonunion wages have been studies of the union–nonunion differential, such as that by Lewis [1963]. This might lead to the belief that our wage equation represents a theory of the union–nonunion differential. But, as will be seen shortly, it is only one aspect of a complete explanation of the determinants of the differential. In other words, Lewis's equation could be viewed as a reduced form from a system of which Eq. 5.3 is a part.

Of course, this effect of nonunion wages on union wages is peculiar to an economy like that of the United States, which is only partially

---

4. See the discussion of the relative merits of value productivity and profits as independent variables in Kuh [1967].

unionized. Our model could be applied to an economy like that of Britain, which is much closer to being totally unionized, but this would require alternative specification of the supply price of labor to the union, W^a. It would then have to be related to the fundamental determinants of the supply of labor, such as demographic factors, etc. The resulting wage equation might be quite different, even though the underlying model would be much the same.

It has been suggested by many economists that in a partially unionized economy spillover effects cause nonunion wages to be related to union wages. If, as our model states, union wages are in turn related to nonunion wages, then clearly a complete system of simultaneous equations is needed to understand the determinants of either union or nonunion wages or both. Rosen [1969] as well as Ashenfelter, Johnson, and Pencavel [1971] has proposed such simultaneous equation models. The contribution of this present study is to strengthen both theoretically and empirically our understanding of the link which the behavior of unions and their employers represents in this system. Further study of other links in the system is required if we are to be able to answer such basic policy problems as: What is the effect of unions on inflation?

Data Appendix

Most of the data series on which the results of Chapter 7 are based are listed in this appendix. Series that are either easily available in published documents or which are confidential have not been listed.

Heavy use was made throughout this study of a Xerox copy of page proofs of U.S. Department of Labor, Bureau of Labor Statistics Bulletin No. 1312–7. The proofs were kindly supplied by the Boston regional office of the Bureau. The September 1969 issue of the *Survey of Current Business* was used to extend all series obtained from that source through June 1969.

The following series have not been listed: all employees, production workers, average weekly hours of production workers, average hourly earnings of production workers. They may be found in the Labor Statistics Bulletin. Other data series which have not been listed include the utilization indices of the Federal Reserve Board, the Wharton utilization index (used for one industry—S.I.C. 34), and the Eckstein–Wyss output price indices. The Federal Reserve Board utilization indices and the Eckstein–Wyss price indices remained confidential when this was written, whereas the Wharton utilization index may be easily obtained from work sheets available at the Economics Research Unit, Wharton School of Finance and Commerce, University of Pennsylvania.

In what follows, sources will be given for the data listed in the tables and for related data that have not been listed.

Table A–1 (pp. 95–97).
Overtime Hours

Figures for 1956.1 through 1969.2 were obtained from proofs for Bulletin 1312–7 and the September 1969 issue of the *Survey of*

Current Business. Extrapolated figures for 1947.1 through 1955.4 were obtained by applying the equations developed in Chapter 6 to quarterly series, not seasonally adjusted, for average weekly hours of production workers in Bulletin 1312–7 and the September 1969 issue of *Survey*. Because the earlier data were not used in the study, the combined series is listed only from 1953.2 on.

Table A–2 (pp. 97–99).
Average Hourly Earnings Excluding Overtime

The point of departure for each of the eight industries was quarterly averages of gross average hourly earnings of production workers obtained from Bulletin 1312.7 and the September 1969 *Survey of Current Business*. These were adjusted for overtime by means of the overtime factor described in Chapter 6, constructed from the data in Table A–1.

Table A–3 (pp. 99–102).
Gross Output per Man Hour at Full Capacity

The definition of gross output of production workers per man hour at full capacity appears in section 6.5. The estimates are based on estimates of Eq. 6.8 presented in Table 6.6. The dependent variable in those equations was the logarithm of the ratio of an index of capacity output over an index of current man hours of production workers. The capacity indices in seven out of eight industries were unpublished indices obtained from the Board of Governors of the Federal Reserve System. Their method of construction is similar to that for the aggregate Federal Reserve Board index of capacity, which is explained in de Leeuw [1966] and Enzler [1967]. The capacity index used for S.I.C. 34 (Fabricated Metal Products) was the Wharton index, taken from a work sheet supplied by the Economics Research Unit, Wharton School of Finance and Commerce, University of Pennsylvania. This work sheet updates the figures published in Klein and Summers [1966].

The indices of man hours of production workers were constructed from figures for number of production workers and average weekly hours of production workers in Bulletin 1312–7 and the September 1969 *Survey of Current Business*.

The independent variables in Eq. 6.8 were seasonal dummies, a capacity utilization index and between four and five time trend variables. The sources for the utilization indices are the same as for the capacity indices. The time trends are identified in Table 6.8. Their construction was described in section 6.5.

Table A–4 (pp. 102–104).
Value Productivity at Full Capacity

These series were obtained by multiplying the physical productivity series of Table A–3 times the Eckstein–Wyss output price indices, whose construction is described in Eckstein and Wyss [1970].

Tables A–5 (pp. 104–106) and A–6 (p. 106).
Seasonally Adjusted Quarterly Layoff Rates

The sources of the nonseasonally adjusted series on which these series are based will be described first. Figures from 1958.1 through 1969.2 are quarterly averages of figures published in Bulletin 1312–7 and the September 1969 *Survey of Current Business*. Figures from 1950.1 through 1957.4 were constructed by extrapolating the 1957 S.I.C. series based on actual values of the 1947 S.I.C. series for the same turnover rates and the same industries. The method is described in Chapter 6. Monthly 1947 S.I.C. series running from January 1950 through July 1961 were collected from every other issue of the *Monthly Labor Review* from 1950 through 1961.

Unadjusted series were used in order to generate the extrapolations. Then, the merged series of extrapolated and actual values were seasonally adjusted with a ratio to moving average program. The seasonal factors generated by the program are listed in Table A–6, while the seasonally adjusted series are listed from 1953.2 through 1969.2 in Table A–5.

Table A–7 (pp. 107–108).
The Nonunion Wage and the Cost of Living

The construction of the nonunion wage series is explained in Section 6.6. The raw materials that went into it consisted first of unpublished quarterly, seasonally adjusted figures for compensation of all employees and man hours of all employees in trade, services, and government enterprises. These figures were generously provided by John Coleman, Office of Business Economics, and Jerome Mark, Bureau of Labor Statistics, respectively. The rate of change of the nonunion compensation per man hour figure obtained from these figures was then adjusted for changes in social security and unemployment compensation taxes and in overtime hours, in a manner suggested by an unpublished study by the author. The estimates taken from that study were that an increase of one point in either tax rate raises the current rate of change of compensation per man-hour 0.20 point, and that an increase of one hour in average overtime raises the same current rate of change 0.59 point. Data on the two tax rates were obtained from the data bank of the FRB-M.I.T.-Penn. econometric model. A series on average overtime in manufacturing published in Bulletin 1312-7 and the September 1969 *Survey of Current Business* was used as a proxy for overtime in the nonunion sector.

The cost-of-living index used in this study was taken from the Department of Commerce, Office of Business Statistics, *Business Statistics, 1969*, and the December 1969 *Survey of Current Business.*

TABLE A-1
AVERAGE WEEKLY OVERTIME HOURS, PRODUCTION WORKERS EXCLUDING OVERTIME
NSA
1953-2 THROUGH 1969-2

DATE	SIC 32	SIC 33	SIC 34	SIC 35
532	3.285	2.896	3.998	4.035
533	3.103	2.801	3.138	3.408
534	3.175	2.272	3.125	3.439
541	2.876	1.506	2.563	2.798
542	2.756	1.324	2.382	2.243
543	2.969	1.631	2.529	2.220
544	3.422	1.989	3.093	2.326
551	3.265	2.547	3.142	2.691
552	3.722	3.023	3.176	3.396
553	3.837	2.961	3.535	3.378
554	3.950	3.467	3.918	4.213
561	3.200	3.033	2.900	4.133
562	3.333	2.833	2.800	3.900
563	3.333	2.767	3.033	3.767
564	3.233	2.600	3.500	3.800
571	2.733	2.367	2.800	3.400
572	2.833	2.000	2.767	2.967
573	3.033	2.000	3.000	2.567
574	2.733	1.400	2.567	2.067
581	2.123	1.033	1.667	1.733
582	2.533	1.067	1.733	1.700
583	3.133	1.567	2.300	1.767
584	3.200	1.833	2.633	2.067
591	3.100	2.333	2.333	2.600
592	3.900	2.900	2.967	3.167
593	4.033	2.667	3.200	2.967
594	3.333	2.533	2.767	3.000
601	2.667	2.433	2.833	3.067
602	3.200	1.767	2.500	2.867
603	3.433	1.567	2.733	2.533
604	3.000	1.333	2.200	2.233
611	2.500	1.300	1.733	2.100
612	3.167	1.700	2.233	2.367
613	3.633	2.233	2.800	2.567
614	3.300	2.233	2.900	2.900
621	2.733	2.567	2.600	3.067
622	3.567	2.200	2.933	3.333
623	3.900	2.033	3.100	3.067
624	3.367	2.167	2.967	2.933
631	2.867	2.400	2.633	3.033
632	3.733	3.067	2.900	3.067
633	4.067	2.633	3.300	3.233
634	3.900	2.567	3.300	3.467
641	3.367	2.767	2.900	3.667
642	4.000	3.000	3.300	3.967
643	4.233	3.533	3.667	3.833
644	3.967	3.500	3.733	4.100
651	3.500	3.833	3.767	4.433
652	4.200	4.167	3.833	4.500
653	4.600	3.800	4.000	4.467
654	4.500	3.433	4.433	5.133
661	4.167	3.833	4.200	5.533
662	4.767	4.133	4.533	5.733
663	4.733	4.200	4.700	5.433
664	4.267	4.000	4.500	5.533
671	3.567	3.467	3.733	5.033

672	4.100	2.900	3.667	4.333
673	4.667	3.100	3.900	4.100
674	4.300	3.300	3.800	4.267
681	3.733	3.767	3.567	4.000
682	4.567	4.167	3.767	3.667
683	4.900	3.733	4.467	3.867
684	4.833	3.700	4.667	4.367
691	4.367	3.967	3.967	4.567
692	4.867	4.133	4.200	4.500

TABLE A-1, CONTINUED
AVERAGE WEEKLY OVERTIME HOURS, PRODUCTION WORKERS
EXCLUDING OVERTIME
NSA
1953-2 THROUGH 1969-2

DATE	SIC 36	SIC 26	SIC 28	SIC 30
532	2.674	4.848	2.078	2.810
533	2.324	4.945	2.108	2.142
534	2.025	4.708	2.030	1.667
541	1.489	3.961	2.001	1.544
542	1.302	3.914	1.875	1.944
543	1.722	4.420	1.989	1.857
544	2.250	4.534	2.030	3.113
551	2.155	4.458	2.085	3.348
552	2.348	4.560	2.053	4.438
553	2.167	5.224	2.175	3.583
554	3.402	5.474	2.326	4.113
561	2.533	4.500	2.033	2.100
562	2.500	4.300	2.067	1.767
563	2.467	4.633	2.100	2.033
564	2.933	4.600	2.067	2.300
571	2.300	4.200	1.967	2.033
572	1.933	4.033	2.000	1.967
573	1.933	4.533	2.067	2.433
574	1.500	4.000	1.967	1.933
581	1.000	3.467	1.733	1.233
582	0.933	3.467	1.833	1.500
583	1.667	4.233	2.000	2.067
584	2.133	4.300	2.100	2.700
591	2.000	4.267	2.200	3.400
592	2.133	4.567	2.567	3.633
593	2.400	4.867	2.633	4.200
594	2.367	4.467	2.433	2.933
601	2.067	4.200	2.333	2.667
602	1.600	4.033	2.600	2.300
603	1.833	4.233	2.333	2.533
604	1.900	3.800	2.100	1.967
611	1.600	3.600	2.067	1.767
612	1.600	4.033	2.267	2.433
613	2.000	4.633	2.433	3.067
614	2.400	4.633	2.500	3.233
621	2.133	4.200	2.500	2.867
622	2.167	4.333	2.667	3.267
623	2.200	4.667	2.567	3.100
624	2.333	4.467	2.400	3.067
631	1.900	4.200	2.367	2.867
632	1.867	4.233	2.767	2.600
633	2.133	4.833	2.567	3.233
634	2.200	4.633	2.400	3.233
641	1.867	4.300	2.500	2.700
642	2.067	4.500	2.733	3.367
643	2.400	5.067	2.833	3.900

Data Appendix

644	2.733	5.000	2.700	3.800
651	2.533	4.633	2.733	3.967
652	2.467	4.600	3.067	3.700
653	2.700	5.300	3.100	4.067
654	3.400	5.633	3.000	4.700
661	3.300	5.167	3.100	4.367
662	3.400	5.533	3.500	4.333
663	3.367	5.667	3.400	4.333
664	3.367	5.500	3.300	4.467
671	2.567	4.867	2.967	3.567
672	2.233	4.700	2.967	3.567
673	2.433	5.200	3.000	4.200
674	2.800	5.167	2.967	4.467
681	2.333	4.933	3.033	3.967
682	2.267	4.933	3.233	3.833
683	3.067	5.667	3.400	4.467
684	3.033	5.733	3.400	4.500
691	2.800	5.400	3.333	4.100
692	2.800	5.367	3.433	4.167

TABLE A-2
AVERAGE HOURLY EARNINGS OF PRODUCTION WORKERS
EXCLUDING OVERTIME
NSA
1953-2 THROUGH 1969-2

DATE	SIC 32	SIC 33	SIC 34	SIC 35
532	1.641	1.961	1.731	1.852
533	1.676	2.027	1.766	1.880
534	1.684	2.023	1.786	1.905
541	1.686	2.027	1.806	1.925
542	1.695	2.032	1.813	1.937
543	1.714	2.073	1.823	1.953
544	1.725	2.084	1.841	1.967
551	1.743	2.095	1.859	1.966
552	1.764	2.110	1.865	1.980
553	1.794	2.220	1.896	2.002
554	1.814	2.224	1.917	2.039
561	1.841	2.241	1.935	2.060
562	1.874	2.256	1.957	2.081
563	1.899	2.279	1.983	2.115
564	1.931	2.362	2.029	2.150
571	1.954	2.394	2.044	2.175
572	1.961	2.403	2.073	2.198
573	1.989	2.484	2.106	2.227
574	2.031	2.501	2.136	2.265
581	2.037	2.522	2.164	2.290
582	2.035	2.547	2.192	2.307
583	2.070	2.637	2.207	2.315
584	2.062	2.665	2.225	2.343
591	2.103	2.696	2.258	2.372
592	2.124	2.728	2.275	2.390
593	2.130	2.602	2.272	2.397
594	2.156	2.653	2.283	2.426
601	2.185	2.767	2.332	2.446
602	2.191	2.751	2.354	2.462
603	2.198	2.731	2.367	2.476
604	2.221	2.738	2.384	2.498
611	2.226	2.782	2.404	2.524
612	2.243	2.819	2.414	2.540
613	2.255	2.841	2.404	2.540
614	2.271	2.890	2.431	2.564
621	2.294	2.918	2.451	2.585

622	2.301	2.901	2.459	2.604
623	2.315	2.880	2.464	2.611
624	2.337	2.891	2.477	2.640
631	2.359	2.920	2.496	2.663
632	2.361	2.961	2.512	2.672
633	2.378	2.945	2.510	2.679
634	2.382	2.951	2.533	2.708
641	2.391	2.967	2.560	2.728
642	2.406	2.989	2.575	2.746
643	2.428	3.007	2.574	2.749
644	2.441	3.005	2.576	2.764
651	2.452	3.023	2.610	2.784
652	2.479	3.039	2.633	2.791
653	2.495	3.049	2.634	2.803
654	2.532	3.059	2.667	2.836
661	2.543	3.099	2.692	2.863
662	2.569	3.131	2.715	2.885
663	2.585	3.140	2.732	2.902
664	2.629	3.156	2.780	2.953
671	2.648	3.164	2.813	2.986
672	2.665	3.187	2.838	3.013
673	2.691	3.234	2.853	3.042
674	2.733	3.279	2.888	3.085
681	2.767	3.327	2.961	3.154
682	2.833	3.368	2.994	3.196
683	2.858	3.412	3.013	3.215
684	2.888	3.474	3.067	3.281
691	2.916	3.533	3.117	3.325
692	2.988	3.574	3.151	3.375

TABLE A-2, CONTINUED
AVERAGE HOURLY EARNINGS OF PRODUCTION WORKERS
EXCLUDING OVERTIME
NSA
1953-2 THROUGH 1969-2

DATE	SIC 36	SIC 26	SIC 28	SIC 30
532	1.672	1.565	1.752	1.747
533	1.695	1.598	1.800	1.759
534	1.717	1.605	1.756	1.756
541	1.744	1.627	1.806	1.765
542	1.751	1.637	1.838	1.786
543	1.749	1.657	1.868	1.788
544	1.758	1.671	1.857	1.821
551	1.769	1.685	1.872	1.836
552	1.779	1.706	1.915	1.849
553	1.802	1.729	1.948	1.872
554	1.803	1.741	1.955	1.916
561	1.843	1.770	1.984	1.949
562	1.876	1.799	2.026	1.960
563	1.902	1.844	2.064	1.986
564	1.963	1.863	2.078	2.004
571	1.967	1.883	2.096	2.023
572	1.979	1.902	2.131	2.018
573	1.982	1.943	2.175	2.069
574	2.028	1.966	2.181	2.119
581	2.073	1.980	2.206	2.102
582	2.088	2.003	2.217	2.109
583	2.077	2.016	2.264	2.148
584	2.098	2.027	2.281	2.168
591	2.130	2.047	2.289	2.180
592	2.134	2.051	2.302	2.146

TABLE A-3, CONTINUED
GROSS OUTPUT PER MANHOUR AT FULL CAPACITY
PRODUCTION WORKERS
1953-2 THROUGH 1969-2

DATE	SIC 36	SIC 26	SIC 28	SIC 30
532	1.305	1.208	1.701	1.191
533	1.320	1.218	1.728	1.202
534	1.334	1.229	1.756	1.213
541	1.349	1.239	1.784	1.224
542	1.364	1.250	1.812	1.235
543	1.379	1.261	1.841	1.246
544	1.394	1.272	1.871	1.258
551	1.409	1.283	1.901	1.269
552	1.425	1.294	1.931	1.281
553	1.440	1.305	1.962	1.296
554	1.456	1.316	1.994	1.311
561	1.472	1.328	2.035	1.327
562	1.488	1.341	2.077	1.342
563	1.488	1.353	2.120	1.358
564	1.498	1.366	2.164	1.374
571	1.508	1.378	2.209	1.390
572	1.518	1.391	2.255	1.407
573	1.527	1.404	2.302	1.423
574	1.537	1.417	2.350	1.440
581	1.547	1.430	2.399	1.457
582	1.557	1.444	2.448	1.474
583	1.568	1.457	2.499	1.491
584	1.578	1.471	2.551	1.509
591	1.588	1.484	2.604	1.527
592	1.598	1.498	2.658	1.545
593	1.609	1.512	2.713	1.563
594	1.609	1.525	2.756	1.575
601	1.609	1.538	2.800	1.588
602	1.622	1.551	2.845	1.601
603	1.635	1.564	2.890	1.614
604	1.648	1.577	2.937	1.627
611	1.662	1.590	2.983	1.640
612	1.675	1.604	3.031	1.653
613	1.689	1.617	3.079	1.666
614	1.703	1.631	3.128	1.679
621	1.717	1.644	3.178	1.693
622	1.731	1.658	3.229	1.707
623	1.745	1.672	3.281	1.720
624	1.759	1.686	3.333	1.734
631	1.773	1.701	3.386	1.748
632	1.788	1.715	3.440	1.762
633	1.802	1.730	3.495	1.776
634	1.817	1.744	3.551	1.790
641	1.832	1.759	3.599	1.805
642	1.847	1.774	3.647	1.819
643	1.862	1.789	3.656	1.834
644	1.877	1.804	3.746	1.849
651	1.892	1.819	3.797	1.863
652	1.907	1.834	3.848	1.878
653	1.923	1.850	3.900	1.893
654	1.939	1.865	3.952	1.909
661	1.954	1.881	4.005	1.924
662	1.970	1.897	4.059	1.939
663	1.986	1.911	4.114	1.955
664	1.989	1.925	4.170	1.971
671	1.993	1.940	4.226	1.984
672	1.996	1.954	4.283	1.998

673	1.999	1.969	4.341	2.012
674	2.002	1.983	4.399	2.026
681	2.005	1.998	4.458	2.040
682	2.008	2.013	4.519	2.054
683	2.011	2.028	4.579	2.068
684	2.014	2.043	4.641	2.082
691	2.018	2.058	4.704	2.097
692	2.021	2.074	4.767	2.111

TABLE A-4
VALUE PRODUCTIVITY AT FULL CAPACITY,
PRODUCTION WORKERS
1953-2 THROUGH 1969-2

DATE	SIC 32	SIC 33	SIC 34	SIC 35
532	1.105	0.935	0.957	1.031
533	1.130	0.956	0.979	1.048
534	1.140	0.954	0.986	1.053
541	1.149	0.959	0.993	1.061
542	1.162	0.975	1.000	1.069
543	1.175	0.988	1.004	1.072
544	1.186	1.000	1.010	1.073
551	1.196	1.021	1.020	1.083
552	1.213	1.051	1.036	1.095
553	1.236	1.103	1.070	1.123
554	1.260	1.139	1.098	1.147
561	1.292	1.173	1.121	1.161
562	1.312	1.203	1.145	1.185
563	1.342	1.216	1.169	1.211
564	1.379	1.238	1.212	1.254
571	1.404	1.254	1.219	1.281
572	1.432	1.261	1.238	1.301
573	1.448	1.273	1.265	1.328
574	1.472	1.275	1.277	1.360
581	1.504	1.280	1.292	1.382
582	1.525	1.281	1.307	1.399
583	1.543	1.302	1.312	1.411
584	1.565	1.334	1.326	1.432
591	1.589	1.354	1.340	1.464
592	1.613	1.373	1.351	1.488
593	1.635	1.375	1.361	1.511
594	1.649	1.397	1.383	1.522
601	1.667	1.419	1.403	1.536
602	1.678	1.425	1.416	1.553
603	1.690	1.424	1.425	1.567
604	1.700	1.421	1.435	1.582
611	1.705	1.418	1.452	1.596
612	1.723	1.431	1.461	1.608
613	1.736	1.445	1.474	1.621
614	1.744	1.448	1.488	1.635
621	1.762	1.456	1.505	1.653
622	1.771	1.463	1.523	1.669
623	1.779	1.468	1.533	1.683
624	1.792	1.469	1.541	1.694
631	1.792	1.474	1.550	1.707
632	1.798	1.487	1.573	1.723
633	1.807	1.500	1.603	1.741
634	1.826	1.523	1.624	1.758
641	1.838	1.541	1.641	1.781
642	1.855	1.560	1.654	1.801
643	1.872	1.576	1.668	1.823
644	1.885	1.613	1.689	1.847

593	2.140	2.082	2.362	2.193
594	2.164	2.100	2.380	2.201
601	2.200	2.115	2.392	2.233
602	2.219	2.135	2.402	2.245
603	2.225	2.168	2.451	2.252
604	2.256	2.187	2.467	2.283
611	2.284	2.201	2.474	2.282
612	2.254	2.215	2.485	2.287
613	2.296	2.236	2.526	2.313
614	2.299	2.246	2.537	2.325
621	2.319	2.264	2.543	2.324
622	2.335	2.271	2.545	2.341
623	2.340	2.295	2.583	2.358
624	2.359	2.312	2.605	2.368
631	2.380	2.328	2.615	2.376
632	2.394	2.340	2.620	2.380
633	2.393	2.367	2.658	2.376
634	2.415	2.385	2.679	2.399
641	2.440	2.398	2.685	2.413
642	2.444	2.413	2.692	2.425
643	2.441	2.440	2.737	2.445
644	2.442	2.451	2.751	2.458
651	2.470	2.476	2.756	2.473
652	2.491	2.490	2.763	2.470
653	2.494	2.516	2.803	2.505
654	2.507	2.527	2.826	2.511
661	2.519	2.551	2.825	2.516
662	2.526	2.576	2.839	2.526
663	2.539	2.607	2.853	2.548
664	2.581	2.630	2.922	2.564
671	2.632	2.661	2.941	2.590
672	2.685	2.688	2.971	2.549
673	2.701	2.738	3.021	2.611
674	2.739	2.768	3.052	2.709
681	2.792	2.800	3.081	2.722
682	2.814	2.842	3.116	2.752
683	2.820	2.894	3.161	2.803
684	2.895	2.927	3.204	2.841
691	2.939	2.959	3.243	2.866
692	2.964	3.006	3.255	2.890

TABLE A-3
GROSS OUTPUT PER MANHOUR AT FULL CAPACITY
PRODUCTION WORKERS
1953-2 THROUGH 1969-2

DATE	SIC 32	SIC 33	SIC 34	SIC 35
532	1.305	1.137	1.124	1.235
533	1.312	1.144	1.129	1.240
534	1.320	1.152	1.135	1.245
541	1.327	1.159	1.141	1.249
542	1.335	1.166	1.147	1.254
543	1.343	1.174	1.152	1.259
544	1.350	1.181	1.158	1.264
551	1.358	1.189	1.164	1.269
552	1.366	1.196	1.170	1.274
553	1.374	1.204	1.176	1.278
554	1.382	1.211	1.187	1.283
561	1.395	1.219	1.198	1.288
562	1.409	1.227	1.209	1.293
563	1.424	1.235	1.220	1.298
564	1.438	1.244	1.232	1.312
571	1.452	1.252	1.244	1.326

572	1.467	1.260	1.255	1.340
573	1.482	1.269	1.267	1.355
574	1.496	1.278	1.279	1.369
581	1.511	1.286	1.291	1.384
582	1.527	1.295	1.303	1.399
583	1.542	1.304	1.315	1.414
584	1.557	1.313	1.328	1.429
591	1.573	1.321	1.340	1.444
592	1.589	1.330	1.353	1.459
593	1.605	1.339	1.364	1.475
594	1.615	1.348	1.375	1.486
601	1.626	1.358	1.387	1.497
602	1.637	1.366	1.399	1.508
603	1.648	1.375	1.410	1.519
604	1.659	1.383	1.422	1.530
611	1.670	1.392	1.434	1.541
612	1.681	1.401	1.446	1.552
613	1.693	1.410	1.458	1.564
614	1.704	1.418	1.470	1.575
621	1.715	1.427	1.482	1.587
622	1.727	1.436	1.495	1.598
623	1.738	1.445	1.507	1.610
624	1.750	1.454	1.520	1.622
631	1.762	1.464	1.533	1.633
632	1.773	1.473	1.546	1.645
633	1.785	1.482	1.558	1.657
634	1.797	1.491	1.572	1.670
641	1.809	1.501	1.585	1.682
642	1.821	1.510	1.598	1.694
643	1.834	1.520	1.611	1.707
644	1.846	1.529	1.625	1.719
651	1.858	1.539	1.638	1.732
652	1.871	1.549	1.652	1.744
653	1.883	1.558	1.666	1.757
654	1.896	1.568	1.680	1.770
661	1.908	1.578	1.694	1.783
662	1.923	1.588	1.708	1.796
663	1.938	1.590	1.713	1.809
664	1.953	1.593	1.717	1.822
671	1.968	1.595	1.722	1.822
672	1.983	1.598	1.726	1.822
673	1.998	1.600	1.731	1.822
674	2.014	1.602	1.735	1.822
681	2.029	1.605	1.740	1.822
682	2.045	1.607	1.745	1.822
683	2.061	1.610	1.749	1.822
684	2.077	1.612	1.754	1.822
691	2.093	1.615	1.759	1.822
692	2.109	1.617	1.763	1.822

Data Appendix

651	1.895	1.633	1.717	1.870
652	1.916	1.655	1.746	1.893
653	1.926	1.675	1.768	1.918
654	1.938	1.692	1.788	1.943
661	1.963	1.707	1.813	1.971
662	1.983	1.740	1.846	2.008
663	2.009	1.752	1.866	2.035
664	2.041	1.758	1.884	2.073
671	2.069	1.771	1.894	2.086
672	2.094	1.770	1.904	2.097
673	2.125	1.777	1.920	2.110
674	2.150	1.813	1.938	2.134
681	2.196	1.854	1.964	2.158
682	2.238	1.847	1.987	2.178
683	2.289	1.839	1.998	2.197
684	2.327	1.852	1.986	2.200
691	2.551	1.865	2.060	2.232
692	2.539	2.017	2.085	2.254

TABLE A-4, CONTINUED
VALUE PRODUCTIVITY AT FULL CAPACITY,
PRODUCTION WORKERS
1953-2 THROUGH 1969-2

DATE	SIC 36	SIC 26	SIC 28	SIC 30
532	1.183	1.086	1.665	1.013
533	1.210	1.100	1.706	1.023
534	1.223	1.113	1.733	1.038
541	1.239	1.116	1.758	1.050
542	1.255	1.122	1.784	1.061
543	1.265	1.136	1.814	1.077
544	1.287	1.136	1.842	1.099
551	1.305	1.152	1.868	1.167
552	1.315	1.174	1.900	1.190
553	1.330	1.199	1.905	1.250
554	1.352	1.239	1.945	1.282
561	1.372	1.270	1.977	1.303
562	1.403	1.305	2.025	1.319
563	1.412	1.324	2.077	1.340
564	1.443	1.342	2.132	1.361
571	1.480	1.362	2.188	1.362
572	1.499	1.376	2.241	1.382
573	1.519	1.397	2.297	1.418
574	1.535	1.416	2.354	1.441
581	1.548	1.430	2.405	1.459
582	1.560	1.445	2.458	1.479
583	1.570	1.457	2.492	1.493
584	1.572	1.469	2.542	1.506
591	1.591	1.477	2.590	1.521
592	1.606	1.497	2.636	1.537
593	1.664	1.519	2.695	1.484
594	1.657	1.532	2.742	1.462
601	1.656	1.560	2.786	1.503
602	1.659	1.582	2.836	1.528
603	1.661	1.598	2.888	1.569
604	1.667	1.609	2.926	1.572
611	1.677	1.607	2.950	1.555
612	1.675	1.573	2.993	1.571
613	1.681	1.578	3.020	1.577
614	1.685	1.614	3.057	1.571
621	1.690	1.636	3.097	1.554
622	1.658	1.666	3.137	1.557

623	1.702	1.669	3.176	1.567
624	1.708	1.670	3.224	1.589
631	1.709	1.679	3.270	1.617
632	1.718	1.697	3.301	1.627
633	1.730	1.716	3.352	1.644
634	1.744	1.734	3.402	1.662
641	1.760	1.751	3.449	1.676
642	1.772	1.751	3.495	1.664
643	1.785	1.765	3.546	1.664
644	1.793	1.783	3.592	1.672
651	1.805	1.799	3.646	1.693
652	1.803	1.825	3.704	1.727
653	1.829	1.847	3.761	1.756
654	1.840	1.871	3.822	1.765
661	1.866	1.898	3.868	1.787
662	1.894	1.932	3.930	1.850
663	1.913	1.966	4.002	1.851
664	1.939	1.985	4.072	1.868
671	1.957	2.006	4.147	1.901
672	1.965	2.029	4.217	1.925
673	1.973	2.056	4.261	1.973
674	1.987	2.083	4.319	2.031
681	2.014	2.108	4.376	2.059
682	2.025	2.109	4.431	2.082
683	2.037	2.119	4.482	2.101
684	2.045	2.141	4.536	2.120
691	2.030	2.191	4.602	2.114
692	2.053	2.234	4.647	2.146

TABLE A-5
QUARTERLY LAYOFF RATE
SA
1953-2 THROUGH 1969-2

DATE	SIC 32	SIC 33	SIC 34	SIC 35
532	0.0370	0.0215	0.0416	0.0339
533	0.0360	0.0361	0.0586	0.0429
534	0.0507	0.0665	0.0812	0.0472
541	0.0557	0.0868	0.1063	0.0730
542	0.0571	0.0686	0.0970	0.0691
543	0.0472	0.0440	0.0804	0.0505
544	0.0405	0.0370	0.0647	0.0494
551	0.0331	0.0262	0.0492	0.0349
552	0.0339	0.0178	0.0553	0.0273
553	0.0371	0.0170	0.0550	0.0262
554	0.0312	0.0161	0.0519	0.0230
561	0.0371	0.0273	0.0772	0.0286
562	0.0470	0.0311	0.0792	0.0339
563	0.0498	0.0261	0.0595	0.0307
564	0.0458	0.0209	0.0536	0.0301
571	0.0515	0.0350	0.0519	0.0386
572	0.0511	0.0418	0.0642	0.0509
573	0.0467	0.0401	0.0639	0.0446
574	0.0632	0.0801	0.0796	0.0858
581	0.0969	0.1420	0.1237	0.1211
582	0.0893	0.0986	0.1018	0.0972
583	0.0538	0.0569	0.0750	0.0545
584	0.0533	0.0337	0.0708	0.0449
591	0.0463	0.0265	0.0638	0.0387
592	0.0399	0.0219	0.0594	0.0313
593	0.0612	0.0402	0.0730	0.0361
594	0.0627	0.0455	0.1149	0.0652
601	0.0567	0.0466	0.0744	0.0487

602	0.0715	0.1096	0.0896	0.0575
603	0.0746	0.0991	0.0879	0.0577
604	0.0846	0.1074	0.1131	0.0694
611	0.0803	0.0890	0.1237	0.0711
612	0.0632	0.0438	0.0763	0.0554
613	0.0587	0.0363	0.0730	0.0433
614	0.0627	0.0419	0.0726	0.0417
621	0.0628	0.0307	0.0706	0.0337
622	0.0646	0.0998	0.0606	0.0355
623	0.0710	0.0726	0.0730	0.0337
624	0.0713	0.0555	0.0671	0.0374
631	0.0602	0.0371	0.0638	0.0399
632	0.0495	0.0280	0.0594	0.0366
633	0.0551	0.0657	0.0610	0.0281
634	0.0627	0.0446	0.0616	0.0288
641	0.0559	0.0265	0.0551	0.0287
642	0.0440	0.0280	0.0557	0.0240
643	0.0477	0.0206	0.0510	0.0241
644	0.0548	0.0209	0.0542	0.0203
651	0.0480	0.0138	0.0396	0.0175
652	0.0426	0.0158	0.0436	0.0167
653	0.0392	0.0333	0.0490	0.0233
654	0.0439	0.0519	0.0377	0.0182
661	0.0375	0.0159	0.0338	0.0150
662	0.0344	0.0134	0.0436	0.0125
663	0.0392	0.0216	0.0370	0.0200
664	0.0439	0.0228	0.0359	0.0139
671	0.0524	0.0350	0.0493	0.0225
672	0.0509	0.0365	0.0509	0.0230
673	0.0392	0.0324	0.0470	0.0241
674	0.0360	0.0237	0.0349	0.0214
681	0.0454	0.0223	0.0435	0.0250
682	0.0316	0.0183	0.0363	0.0251
683	0.0294	0.0588	0.0440	0.0241
684	0.0282	0.0282	0.0313	0.0182
691	0.0305	0.0148	0.0329	0.0175
692	0.0261	0.0158	0.0412	0.0178

TABLE A-5
QUARTERLY LAYOFF RATE
SA
1953-2 THROUGH 1969-2

DATE	SIC 36	SIC 26	SIC 28	SIC 30
532	0.0194	0.0209	0.0227	0.0257
533	0.0290	0.0175	0.0286	0.0494
534	0.0673	0.0256	0.0306	0.0825
541	0.0583	0.0289	0.0382	0.0617
542	0.0668	0.0260	0.0314	0.0641
543	0.0436	0.0357	0.0309	0.0572
544	0.0442	0.0220	0.0245	0.0407
551	0.0359	0.0183	0.0216	0.0343
552	0.0349	0.0171	0.0213	0.0360
553	0.0358	0.0212	0.0182	0.0356
554	0.0302	0.0229	0.0217	0.0281
561	0.0421	0.0245	0.0228	0.0513
562	0.0402	0.0248	0.0253	0.0632
563	0.0263	0.0200	0.0297	0.0356
564	0.0335	0.0229	0.0236	0.0357
571	0.0386	0.0395	0.0239	0.0468
572	0.0402	0.0324	0.0240	0.0481
573	0.0436	0.0285	0.0309	0.0434
574	0.0760	0.0390	0.0331	0.0531

SIC				
581	0.0897	0.0430	0.0544	0.1074
582	0.0731	0.0513	0.0413	0.0864
583	0.0459	0.0282	0.0301	0.0461
584	0.0386	0.0312	0.0306	0.0383
591	0.0311	0.0251	0.0215	0.0369
592	0.0280	0.0257	0.0207	0.0432
593	0.0372	0.0271	0.0212	0.0412
594	0.0456	0.0338	0.0275	0.0584
601	0.0417	0.0314	0.0228	0.0507
602	0.0511	0.0308	0.0253	0.0704
603	0.0484	0.0350	0.0301	0.0654
604	0.0575	0.0439	0.0326	0.0794
611	0.0533	0.0368	0.0316	0.0747
612	0.0391	0.0334	0.0260	0.0409
613	0.0397	0.0339	0.0268	0.0473
614	0.0337	0.0296	0.0255	0.0475
621	0.0302	0.0287	0.0253	0.0361
622	0.0270	0.0295	0.0222	0.0364
623	0.0434	0.0339	0.0268	0.0594
624	0.0396	0.0321	0.0275	0.0484
631	0.0444	0.0332	0.0228	0.0421
632	0.0371	0.0295	0.0237	0.0420
633	0.0434	0.0294	0.0234	0.0582
634	0.0426	0.0296	0.0255	0.0520
641	0.0453	0.0278	0.0240	0.0421
642	0.0371	0.0257	0.0222	0.0443
643	0.0384	0.0260	0.0223	0.0509
644	0.0297	0.0262	0.0224	0.0465
651	0.0240	0.0242	0.0228	0.0283
652	0.0230	0.0231	0.0199	0.0386
653	0.0310	0.0271	0.0178	0.0497
654	0.0149	0.0194	0.0194	0.0301
661	0.0115	0.0161	0.0202	0.0206
662	0.0130	0.0167	0.0145	0.0250
663	0.0211	0.0169	0.0156	0.0364
664	0.0159	0.0144	0.0173	0.0246
671	0.0382	0.0161	0.0215	0.0387
672	0.0320	0.0205	0.0153	0.0329
673	0.0310	0.0226	0.0201	0.0400
674	0.0258	0.0160	0.0163	0.0265
681	0.0266	0.0179	0.0164	0.0232
682	0.0210	0.0154	0.0115	0.0250
683	0.0248	0.0203	0.0145	0.0327
684	0.0208	0.0118	0.0133	0.0237
691	0.0195	0.0134	0.0126	0.0206
692	0.0170	0.0154	0.0107	0.0250

TABLE A-6
SEASONAL FACTORS, QUARTERLY LAYOFFS

SIC	FIRST QUARTER	SECOND QUARTER	THIRD QUARTER	FOURTH QUARTER
32	0.8728	1.3746	1.2236	0.7834
33	1.0601	1.2175	0.9808	0.9104
34	0.9666	1.2115	0.9994	0.9194
35	1.2481	1.0449	0.8020	1.0681
36	0.8877	1.0015	1.2401	0.9908
26	0.8965	1.2830	1.1295	0.8445
28	1.2646	0.7656	1.1153	1.0195
30	0.8591	1.1362	1.2120	0.9127

TABLE A-7
NONUNION WAGE AND COST OF LIVING
NSA
1953-2 THROUGH 1969-2

532	1.415175	92.966614
533	1.433501	93.699982
534	1.445204	93.799942
541	1.460101	93.733307
542	1.468934	93.633301
543	1.476643	93.699936
544	1.478749	93.299942
551	1.494019	93.199936
552	1.518785	93.133301
553	1.534737	93.466614
554	1.539900	93.599930
561	1.569798	93.433243
562	1.607980	94.133301
563	1.628839	95.333252
564	1.648589	96.033264
571	1.680806	96.633301
572	1.699714	97.566635
573	1.725828	98.599930
574	1.747441	98.966614
581	1.769418	99.999893
582	1.781594	100.733307
583	1.799562	100.866608
584	1.809990	100.866608
591	1.829152	100.833252
592	1.840014	101.199936
593	1.864054	101.833252
594	1.889949	102.333252
601	1.912655	102.333252
602	1.931661	102.966614
603	1.948872	103.233307
604	1.961222	103.799942
611	1.975521	103.866608
612	1.994526	103.899979
613	2.017392	104.433243
614	2.026499	104.566635
621	2.047127	104.766602
622	2.075322	105.233307
623	2.089012	105.699936
624	2.119923	105.933243
631	2.138221	106.099930
632	2.154220	106.333252
633	2.169606	107.099930
634	2.194529	107.399979
641	2.231820	107.666565
642	2.245427	107.866608
643	2.280744	108.299942
644	2.303417	108.666565
651	2.306801	108.933243
652	2.334732	109.666565
653	2.371020	110.133301
654	2.408924	110.666565
661	2.441085	111.533264
662	2.475480	112.666565
663	2.514087	113.733307
664	2.561234	114.599930
671	2.620757	114.833252
672	2.666574	115.633301
673	2.698730	116.833252

674	2.749031	117.833252
681	2.811357	119.033264
682	2.854279	120.366608
683	2.894160	121.866608
684	2.968535	123.333252
691	3.020734	124.766602
692	3.055634	126.933243

Bibliography

Ashenfelter, Orley A. and George E. Johnson, "Bargaining Theory, Trade Unions, and Industrial Strike Activity," *American Economic Review*, Vol. 59 (March 1969), 35–49.

Ashenfelter, Orley A., George E. Johnson, and John H. Pencavel, "Trade Unions and the Rate of Change of Money Wages in the United States," Working Paper No. 12, Industrial Relations Section, Princeton University, revised January 1971.

Behman, Sara A., "Labor Mobility, Increasing Labor Demand, and Money Wage-Rate Increases in United States Manufacturing," *Review of Economic Studies*, Vol. 31 (December 1964), 253–266.

———, "Wage Determination in a Cyclical Setting" Ph.D. thesis, University of California, Berkeley, California, 1966.

———, "Wage-Determination Process in United States Manufacturing," *Quarterly Journal of Economics*, Vol. 82 (February 1968), 117–143.

Bhatia, Rattan J., "Profits and the Rate of Change in Money Earnings in the United States, 1935–1959," *Economica*, N.S., Vol. 29 (August 1962), 225–262.

Bishop, Robert L., "Game Theoretic Analyses of Bargaining," *Quarterly Journal of Economics*, Vol. 77, (November 1963), 559–602.

———, "A Zeuthen–Hicks Theory of Bargaining," *Econometrica*, Vol. 32 (July 1964), 410–417.

Bowen, William G., *Wage Behavior in the Postwar Period—An Empirical Analysis*. Princeton, N.J.: Princeton University Press, 1960.

Cartter, Allan M., *Theory of Wages and Employment*, Homewood, Ill.: Richard D. Irwin, Inc., 1959.

Chamberlain, Neil W., *A General Theory of Economic Process*, New York: Harper and Brothers, 1955.

Coddington, Alan, "A Theory of the Bargaining Process: Comment," *American Economic Review*, Vol. 56 (June 1966), 522–530.

———, *Theories of the Bargaining Process*, London: Allen and Unwin, 1968.

Cohen, Malcolm S. and Robert M. Solow, "The Behavior of Help-Wanted Advertising," *Review of Economics and Statistics*, Vol. 49 (February 1967).

Cross, J. G., "A Theory of the Bargaining Process," *American Economic Review*, Vol. 55 (March 1965), 67–94.

——, "A Theory of the Bargaining Process: Reply," *American Economic Review*, Vol. 56 (June 1966), 530–533.

Dunlop, John T., *Wage Determination Under Trade Unions*, New York: Macmillan Co., 1944.

Eckstein, Otto and Thomas A. Wilson, "The Determination of Money Wages in American Industry," *Quarterly Journal of Economics*, Vol. 76 (August 1962), 379–414.

Eckstein, Otto and David Wyss, "Industry Price Equations," paper presented to the Federal Reserve Board and Social Science Research Council Conference on "The Econometrics of Price Determination," Washington, D.C., October 1970.

Enzler, Jared J., "Revised Indexes of Manufacturing Capacity and Capacity Utilization," *Federal Reserve Bulletin*, Vol. 53 (July 1967), 1096.

Fellner, William, "Prices and Wages Under Bilateral Monopoly," *Quarterly Journal of Economics*, Vol. 61 (August 1947), 503–532.

——, *Competition Among the Few, Oligopoly and Similar Market Structures* (reprint), New York: Augustus M. Kelley, 1960.

Foldes, Lucien, "A Determinate Model of Bilateral Monopoly," *Economica*, N.S., Vol. 31 (February 1964), 117–131.

Galbraith, John Kenneth, *American Capitalism: A Theory of Countervailing Power*, New York: Houghton Mifflin and Company, 1956.

Garbarino, Joseph William, "Unionism and the General Wage Level," *American Economic Review*, Vol. 40 (December 1950), 893–896.

Gordon, Robert J., "The Incidence of the Corporation Income Tax in Manufacturing, 1925–62," *American Economic Review*, Vol. 57 (September 1967), 731–758.

——, "Incidence of the Corporation Tax in U.S. Manufacturing: Reply," *American Economic Review*, Vol. 58 (December 1968), 1360–1367.

Hamermesh, Daniel S., "Wage Bargains, Threshold Effects and The Phillips Curve," *Quarterly Journal of Economics*, Vol. 84 (August 1970), 501–517.

———, "Market Power, Wage Inflation and the New Industrial State," Working Paper 22, Industrial Relations Section, Princeton University, October 1970.

Hansen, Bent, *A Study in the Theory of Inflation*, London: Allen and Unwin, 1951.

Harsanyi, John C., "Approaches to the Bargaining Problem Before and After the Theory of Games: A Critical Discussion of Zeuthen's, Hicks', and Nash's Theories," *Econometrica*, Vol. 24 (April 1956), 144–157.

———, "Notes on the Bargaining Problem," *Southern Economic Journal*, Vol. 24 (April 1958), 471–482.

———, "On the Rationality Postulates Underlying the Theory of Cooperative Games," *Journal of Conflict Resolution*, Vol. 5 (June 1961), 179–196.

———, "Rationality Postulates for Bargaining Solutions in Cooperative and in Non-Cooperative Games," *Management Science*, Vol. 9 (October 1962), 141–153.

Henderson, A. M., "A Further Note on the Problem of Bilateral Monopoly," *Journal of Political Economy*, Vol. 48 (April 1940), 238–243.

Hicks, John R., *The Theory of Wages*, 2nd ed., London: Macmillan Co., 1963.

Klein, L. R. and R. S. Preston, "Some New Results in the Measurement of Capacity Utilization," *American Economic Review*, Vol. 5 (March 1967), 34–58.

Klein, L. R. and R. Summers, *The Wharton Index of Capacity Utilization*, Studies in Quantitative Economics No. 1. Philadelphia, Pa.: Economics Research Unit, Department of Economics, Wharton School of Finance and Commerce, University of Pennsylvania, 1966.

Kryzaniak, Marian, and Richard A. Musgrave, *The Shifting of the Corporation Income Tax, An Empirical Study of its Short-run Effect upon the Rate of Return*, Baltimore: Johns Hopkins University Press, 1963.

Kuh, Edwin, "A Productivity Theory of Wage Levels—An Alternative to the Phillips Curve," *Review of Economic Studies*, Vol. 34, No. 100 (October 1967).

De Leeuw, Frank, with Frank E. Hopkins and Michael D. Sherman, "A Revised Index of Manufacturing Capacity," *Federal Reserve Bulletin*, Vol. 52 (November 1966).

Leontief, Wassily, "The Pure Theory of the Guaranteed Annual Wage Contract," *Journal of Political Economy*, Vol. 54 (February 1945), 76–79.

Levinson, Harold M., "Postwar Movement of Prices and Wages in Manufacturing Industries," in Joint Economic Committee, *Study of Employment, Growth, and Price Levels*, Study Paper No. 21, Washington, D.C.: U.S. Government Printing Office, 1960.

Lewis, Harold Gregg, *Unionism and Relative Wages in the United States; an Empirical Inquiry*, Chicago: University of Chicago Press, 1963.

Lipsey, Richard G., "The Relation Between Unemployment and the Rate of Change of Money Wage Rates in the United Kingdom, 1862–1957: A Further Analysis," *Economica*, N.S., Vol. 27 (February 1960), 1–31.

Luce, R. Duncan, and Howard Raiffa, *Games and Decisions, Introduction and Critical Survey*, New York: John Wiley & Sons, 1957.

Machlup, F., and Martha Taber, "Bilateral Monopoly, Successive Monopoly, and Vertical Integration," *Economica*, Vol. 27 (May 1960), 101–119.

Marshall, Alfred, *Principles of Economics*, 8th ed., New York: Macmillan Co., 1920.

McGuire, Timothy W. and Leonard A. Rapping, "Interindustry Wage Change Dispersion and the 'Spillover' Hypothesis," *American Economic Review*, Vol. 56 (June 1966), 493–501.

———, "The Determination of Money Wages in American Industry: Comment," *Quarterly Journal of Economics*, Vol. 81 (November 1967), 684–689.

———, "The Role of Market Variables and Key Bargains in the Manufacturing Wage Determination Process," *Journal of Political Economy*, Vol. 76 (September/October 1968), 1015–1036.

———, "The Supply of Labor and Manufacturing Wage Determination in the United States: An Empirical Examination," unpublished MS., Carnegie-Mellon University, 1968.

De Menil, George, and Jared J. Enzler, "Prices and Wages in the FRB-M.I.T.-Penn Econometric Model," paper presented to the Federal Reserve Board and Social Science Research Council Conference on "The Econometrics of Price Determination," Washington, D.C., October 1970.

Modigliani, Franco, "Econometric Models of Stabilization Policies," unpublished paper presented to the Third Far Eastern Meeting of the Econometric Society, June 27, 1968.

Musgrave, Richard A., *The Theory of Public Finance, A Study in Public Economy*, New York: McGraw-Hill Co., 1959.

Nash, John F., Jr., "The Bargaining Problem," *Econometrica*, Vol. 18 (April 1950), 155–162.

———, "Two Person Cooperative Games," *Econometrica*, Vol. 21 (January 1953), 128–140.

Okun, A., "Potential GNP: Its Measurement and Significance," *American Statistical Association*, Proceedings, 1962, 98–104.

Pen, Jan, "A General Theory of Bargaining," *American Economic Review*, Vol. 42 (March 1952), 24–42.

———, *The Wage Rate Under Collective Bargaining* (trans. by T. S. Preston), Cambridge, Mass.: Harvard University Press, 1959.

Perry, George L., *Unemployment, Money Wage Rates, and Inflation*, Cambridge, Mass.: The M.I.T. Press, 1966.

Phelps, Edmund, "Money-Wage Dynamics and Labor Market Equilibrium," *Journal of Political Economy*, Vol. 76 (July 1968), 678–711.

Phillips, A. W., "The Relation Between Unemployment and the Rate of Change of Money Wage Rates in the United Kingdom, 1861–1957," *Economica*, N.S., Vol. 25 (November 1958), 283–299.

Pierson, G., "The Effect of Union Strength on the U.S. 'Phillips Curve,'" *American Economic Review*, Vol. 58, No. 2 (June 1968).

Raiffa, Howard, "Arbitration Schemes for Generalized Two-Person Games," in H. W. Kuhn and A. W. Tucker (eds.), *Contributions to the Theory of Games, II*, Princeton, N.J.: Princeton University Press, 1953.

Rapping, Leonard A., "Monopoly Rents, Wage Rates, and Union Effectiveness," *Quarterly Review of Economics and Business*, Vol. VII (Spring 1967), 31–47.

Rees, Albert, *The Economics of Trade Unions*, Chicago: University of Chicago Press, 1962.

Rees, Albert and Mary T. Hamilton, "The Wage-Price-Productivity Perplex," *Journal of Political Economy*, Vol. 75 (February 1967), 63–70.

Rosen, Sherwin, "Trade Union Power, Threat Effects and the Extent of Organization," *Review of Economic Studies*, Vol. 36 (April 1969).

———, "Unionism and the Occupational Wage Structure in the United States," *International Economic Review*, Vol. II (June 1970).

Ross, Arthur M., *Trade Union Wage Policy*, Berkeley: University of California Press, 1956.

Saraydar, Edward, "Zeuthen's Theory of Bargaining: A Note," *Econometrica*, Vol. 33 (October 1965), 802–813.

Sargan, J. D., "Wages and Prices in the United Kingdom: A Study in Econometric Methodology," in P. E. Hart, G. Mills, and J. K. Whitaker (eds.), *Econometric Analysis for National Economic Planning, Proceedings of the Sixteenth Symposium of the Colston Research Society Held in the University of Bristol, April 6th–9th 1964*, London: Butterworth's, 1964.

Schackle, George L. S., *Expectation in Economics*, Cambridge: Cambridge University Press, 1949.

———, "The Nature of the Bargaining Process," in John T. Dunlop (ed.), *The Theory of Wage Determination; Proceedings of a Conference Held by the International Economic Association*, London: Macmillan Co., 292–314.

Schelling, Thomas C., *The Strategy of Conflict*. Cambridge, Mass.: Harvard University Press, 1960.

Siegal, Sidney and Lawrence E. Fouraker, *Bargaining and Group Decision Making*, New York: McGraw-Hill Co., 1960.

Simler, N. J. and A. Tella, "Labor Reserves and the Phillips Curve," *Review of Economics and Statistics*, Vol. 50, No. 1 (February 1968).

Stahl, Ingolf, "Bargaining Theory: Models of Bilateral Monopoly and Duopoly," mimeographed, Economic Research Institute at the Stockholm School of Economics, July 1971.

Stevens, Carl M., *Strategy and Collective Bargaining Negotiation*, New York: McGraw-Hill Co., 1963.

Sutch, Richard, "Employment, Hours, and Prices in the M.I.T.-FRB Econometric Model," mimeo, M.I.T., April 1967.

Throop, A. W., "The Union-Nonunion Wage Differential and Cost-Push Inflation," *American Economic Review*, Vol. 58, No. 1 (March 1968), 79–99.

Von Neumann, John and Oskar Morgenstern, *Theory of Games and Economic Behavior*, 3rd ed., Princeton, N.J.: Princeton University Press, 1953.

Wachter, Michael L., "Cyclical Variation in the Interindustry Wage Structure," *American Economic Review*, Vol. 60 (March 1970), 75–84.

Wagner, Harvey M., "A Unified Treatment of Bargaining Theory," *Southern Economic Journal*, Vol. 23 (April 1957), 380–397.

———, "Rejoinder on the Bargaining Problem," *Southern Economic Journal*, Vol. 24 (April 1958), 476–482.

Walton, Richard E. and Robert B. McKensie, *A Behavioral Theory of Labor Negotiations: An Analysis of a Social Interaction System*, New York: McGraw-Hill Co., 1965.

Weiss, Leonard W., "Concentration and Labor Earnings," *American Economic Review*, Vol. 56 (March 1966), 96–117.

Zeuthen, F., *Problems of Monopoly and Economic Warfare*, Chapter 4, London: George Routledge and Sons, 1930.

Publications of the Joint Center for Urban Studies

The Joint Center for Urban Studies, a cooperative venture of the Massachusetts Institute of Technology and Harvard University, was founded in 1959 to organize and encourage research on urban and regional problems. Participants have included scholars from the fields of anthropology, architecture, business, city planning, economics, education, engineering, history, law, philosophy, political science, and sociology.

The findings and conclusions of this book are, as with all Joint Center publications, solely the responsibility of the author.

Published by Harvard University Press

The Intellectual versus the City: From Thomas Jefferson to Frank Lloyd Wright, by Morton and Lucia White, 1962

Streetcar Suburbs: The Process of Growth in Boston, 1870–1900, by Sam B. Warner, Jr., 1962

City Politics, by Edward C. Banfield and James Q. Wilson, 1963

Law and Land: Anglo-American Planning Practice, edited by Charles M. Haar, 1964

Location and Land Use: Toward a General Theory of Land Rent, by William Alonso, 1964

Poverty and Progress: Social Mobility in a Nineteenth Century City, by Stephan Thernstrom, 1964

Boston: The Job Ahead, by Martin Meyerson and Edward C. Banfield, 1966

The Myth and Reality of Our Urban Problems, by Raymond Vernon, 1966

Muslim Cities in the Later Middle Ages, by Ira Marvin Lapidus, 1967

The Fragmented Metropolis: Los Angeles, 1850–1930, by Robert M. Fogelson, 1967

Law and Equal Opportunity: A Study of the Massachusetts Commission Against Discrimination, by Leon H. Mayhew, 1968

Varieties of Police Behavior: The Management of Law and Order in Eight Communities, by James Q. Wilson, 1968

The Metropolitan Enigma: Inquiries into the Nature and Dimensions of America's "Urban Crisis," edited by James Q. Wilson, revised edition, 1968

Traffic and The Police: Variations in Law-Enforcement Policy, by John A. Gardiner, 1969

The Influence of Federal Grants: Public Assistance in Massachusetts, by Martha Derthick, 1970

The Arts in Boston, by Bernard Taper, 1970

Families Against the City: Middle Class Homes of Industrial Chicago, 1872–1890, by Richard Sennett, 1970

The Political Economy of Urban Schools, by Martin T. Katzman, 1971

Origins of the Urban School: Public Education in Massachusetts, 1870–1915, by Marvin Lazerson, 1971

Published by The MIT Press

The Image of the City, by Kevin Lynch, 1960

Housing and Economic Progress: A Study of the Housing Experiences of Boston's Middle-Income Families, by Lloyd Rodwin, 1961

The Historian and the City, edited by Oscar Handlin and John Burchard, 1963

The Federal Bulldozer: A Critical Analysis of Urban Renewal, 1949–1962, by Martin Anderson, 1964

The Future of Old Neighborhoods: Rebuilding for a Changing Population, by Bernard J. Frieden, 1964

Man's Struggle for Shelter in an Urbanizing World, by Charles Abrams, 1964

The View from the Road, by Donald Appleyard, Kevin Lynch, and John R. Myer, 1964

The Public Library and the City, edited by Ralph W. Conant, 1965

Regional Development Policy: A Case Study of Venezuela, by John Friedmann, 1966

Urban Renewal: The Record and the Controversy, edited by James Q. Wilson, 1966

Transport Technology for Developing Regions, by Richard M. Soberman, 1966

Computer Methods in the Analysis of Large-Scale Social Systems, edited by James M. Beshers, 1968

Planning Urban Growth and Regional Development: The Experience of the Guayana Program of Venezuela, by Lloyd Rodwin and Associates, 1969

Build a Mill, Build a City, Build a School: Industrialization, Urbanization, and Education in Ciudad Guayana, by Noel F. McGinn and Russell G. Davis, 1969

Land-Use Controls in the United States, by John Delafons, second edition, 1969

Beyond the Melting Pot: The Negroes, Puerto Ricans, Jews, Italians, and Irish of New York City, by Nathan Glazer and Daniel Patrick Moynihan, revised edition, 1970

Bargaining: Monopoly Power versus Union Power, by George de Menil, 1971

The Joint Center also publishes monographs and reports.

Index

Accessions rate, 46
Aggregation, 47, 51, 55
Arbitrator, in game theory, 7–8
Ashenfelter, Orley A., 20n, 88, 89
Atonement, 16

Bargaining,
 atonement in, 16
 government intervention in, 50
 risk in, 15, 16n, 19
 stalemate in, 15
 two-person, 4, 5, 8
Bargaining equations, 77–84
Bargaining models, 1
Bargaining theories, 1, 4–20
Bargaining variables, 1–3, 20, 77
Behman, Sara A., 46
Bishop, Robert L., 6, 9n, 10n, 14–15, 18
Bowen, William G., 31n
Bureau of Labor Statistics, 44, 54, 56, 57, 62, 71, 73, 80, 90, 93

Capacity utilization, 64, 65, 68, 69–70, 90, 91, 92
Capital costs, 30, 40
Capital expansion, 25
Capital plans, 28
Capital stock, 1, 21, 24–25
Capital supply, 1, 21, 44
Chamberlain, Neil W., 16n
Coddington, Alan, 18
Cohen, Malcolm S., 46
Coleman, John, 93
Competition, perfect, 30, 87
Contract curve, 4, 7, 8, 12, 24–26, 33
Cost of living, 37, 38, 49, 73, 77, 82–84, 93, 94
Cross, J. G., 18, 20
Cyclical variation, 42–43, 44, 45, 53, 69, 88

Delay time, 17, 19
Demand curve, 1, 21, 24, 30, 37
Demand pressure, 43, 45
Density function, 74
Dunlop, John T., 21, 22–23, 30

Eckstein, Otto, 2n, 46–48, 62, 86, 88, 90, 92
Eckstein-Wyss index, 90, 92
Efficiency axiom, 8, 14
Elasticity,
 of output, 44n, 62, 63, 68
 of utility functions, 13–14, 26, 41
 of utility increments, 12–14, 24, 27, 33–36
 of wage rate, 36, 38, 50, 79, 80, 81
Employment, 1, 21, 24–25, 28, 31–32, 45; see also Job turnover, Job upgrading, Layoffs, Quit Rate
Enzler, Jared J., 64n, 91
Equilibrium,
 strategies of, 8
 of wage rate, 48–49, 86–87
Expectations,
 in bargaining games, 8
 static, 48–49
Expected earnings, 42–43
Expected profits, 23, 42–43
Expected utility, 15
Expected wage surplus, 23
Expected wages, 48–49

Federal Reserve Board, 64–65, 90, 91, 93
Fellner, William, 26n
Foldes, Lucien, 17–18

Games,
 cooperative, 5
 minimax theorem of, 8
 nonzero sum, 5, 28

Games (continued)
  rational players in, 7–8, 19
  strategies of, 8
  symmetric, 5
  theory of, 4–8, 19, 86
  threat concept of, 5–7
  two-person, 5
  zero sum, 8
Gordon, Robert J., 31n
Government intervention,
  in bargaining, 50
  in monopolies, 10
Growth trends, 69–70, 74

Hamermesh, Daniel S., 2n
Hansen, Bent, 36
Harsanyi, John C., 7n, 9n, 15, 16
Hicks, John R., 6, 16–17, 18, 19–20
Hourly earnings, average, 2, 52–55, 59, 61, 70, 73, 76, 78, 81, 87n, 90, 91
Hours worked, 56–59, 60, 62, 92; *see also* Man hours

Income distribution, 27, 29–30, 39
Industries,
  concentrated, 87
  three-digit, 54–55
  two-digit, 2, 45, 46–48, 51, 53–54, 57, 62, 71, 87n
Irrelevant alternatives axiom, 9–10, 11, 14, 19

Job turnover, 45–46, 70–72, 92
Job upgrading, 49, 52
Johnson, George E., 20n, 88, 89
Johnson, President Lyndon B., 50

Kennedy, President John F., 50
Klein, L. R., 65n, 92
Kryzaniak, Marian, 31n
Kuh, Edwin, 2n, 48–49, 86–87, 88

Labor supply, by unions, 1, 21, 30, 42, 44, 87, 89
Late-shift work, 52–53
Layoffs, 45, 71–72, 73, 75–77, 82, 83, 92
de Leeuw, Frank, 64n, 91
Levinson, Harold M., 31n
Lewis, Harold Gregg, 44n, 88
Limitations of study, 84
Lipsey, Richard G., 36
Luce, R. Duncan, 7n, 13, 14n

Machlup, F., 4n
Man hours, 52, 61, 62–63, 65, 67, 68, 70, 87n, 91, 92, 93; *see also* Hours worked
Mark, Jerome, 93
Massachusetts Institute of Technology (M.I.T.), 93
Maximization,
  joint, 25–26
  of profits, 22, 24, 25, 87
  of rents, 23n
  of utility, 87
  of wages, 23, 25
McGuire, Timothy W., 2n
McKensie, Robert B., 16n
Membership function, 21
Minimax theorem, 8
Models, 1, 16n, 21, 84, 89; *see also* Monopoly, Nash model
Modigliani, Franco, 62
Monopoly,
  bilateral model, 1, 10, 21–28, 29–31, 85, 86
  simple (standard) model, 1, 27n, 29–31, 40
Morgenstern, Oskar, 4, 6
Musgrave, Richard A., 31n

Nash, John F., Jr., 1, 4, 6, 8–14,

Nash, John F., Jr. (continued)
  18–20, 23, 26, 27
Nash model,
  comparative statics of, 29–39
  derivation of, 21–28
  derivation of wage equation in,
    40–50
  empirical validation of, 51–74, 75–85
  general characteristics of, 29–31
  implications of, 86–89
New hire rate, 46

O'Donnell, Edward T., 57
Office of Business Economics, 44, 93
Okun's Law, 62, 63
Output, 1, 21, 24, 30, 31–32, 44n, 62–64, 68, 91
Output price index, 62, 90, 92
Overtime, 52–53, 55–59, 70–71, 73–74, 90–91, 93, 94
  compositional effects on, 59–62
  positive vs. negative, 56
  quarterly equations, 58
  seasonal effects on, 59–62

Pen Jan, 16n
Pencavel, John H., 88, 89
Perry, George L., 2n, 31, 32, 47–48, 86, 88
Phillips, A. W., 36
Phillips curve, 2–3, 36, 75–76, 84, 85, 86
Piece-rate workers, 52
Pierson, G., 2n, 47n, 86
Preston, R. S., 65n
Prices, 1, 21, 24, 29, 49
  effect of profits tax on, 31–32, 39
  effect of wages on, 36–38, 39
  labor demand-vs.-supply price, 82
  markup price equation, 84
Pricing policy, 25, 27

Product-market force, 30–31
Production function, 1, 21, 30, 44n, 65n
Production index, 65
Productivity,
  long-run, 62
  of piece-rate workers, 52
  real, 73–74
  trend rates of, 63–64, 68–69, 74
  value, 44, 73, 80, 81, 83, 84, 88, 92
  and variable construction, 62–70
  and wages, 78
Productivity equations, 67
Profit identity, 27, 29, 37–38, 40
Profit maximization, 22, 24, 25, 87
Profit sharing, 87
Profits, 1, 21, 22, 27, 31, 87, 88
Profits tax, 29, 31–36, 39, 41
Public opinion, 10

Quit rate, 45–46

Raiffa, Howard, 7n, 13, 14, 19
Rapping, Leonard A., 2n, 87n
Rees, Albert, 23n, 30n, 87n
Rehire rate, 46
Rent maximization, 23n
Resources, allocation of, 29–30
Revenue, 26, 30, 40, 44n
Risk, 14, 16n, 19
Rosen, Sherwin, 23n, 88, 89
Ross, Arthur M., 22

Saraydar, Edward, 16n
Sargan, J. D., 48–49, 86, 88
Schackle, George L. S., 16n
Schelling, Thomas C., 5, 8n
Simler, N. J., 47n
Slowdowns, 6
Solow, Robert M., 46
Stalemate, 15

Index

Steel agreement of 1962, 25
Stevens, Carl M., 16n
Strikes, 6, 17, 20, 24, 27, 43, 61, 67, 76, 78
Summers, R., 65n, 92
Sutch Richard, 62
Symmetry axiom, 9, 14

Taber, Martha, 4n
Taxes,
 corporate income, 31–32, 34
 linear, 32, 34, 36, 39, 41
 nonproportional, 34–35
 profits, 29, 31–36, 39, 41
 progressive, 36
 proportional, 38
 social security, 70, 93
 uhemployment, 70, 93
Tella, A., 47n
Threat,
 fixed vs. variable, 5–7, 8, 14, 23, 85
 in game theory, 5–7
 instruments of, 6
Threat point, 7, 10, 12, 16
Throop, A. W., 2n
Time discount rates, 18
Time trends, 65, 66, 72
Transformation invariance axiom, 9–10, 14–15
Transformation, linear, 4, 9, 14, 21–22

Unemployment, 45–46, 62n, 75, 88
Unions,
 demand for information on operations, 25
 as economic institution, 22–23
 influence on wages, 86–88
 labor supply by, 1, 21, 30, 42, 44, 87, 89
 as political institution, 22

University of Pennsylvania, 65n, 93
Utility frontier, 7, 8, 9, 10, 14, 15, 20
Utility function, 1, 4–5, 9, 12–14, 16–17, 21–22, 23, 24, 33, 35–36, 38, 80, 81–82
Utility increments, 7, 9, 10, 12, 14, 24, 27, 33–36
Utility maximization, 87

Variables,
 bargaining, 1–3, 20, 29, 75, 84
 construction of, 2, 52–70
 dependent, 50, 51, 58, 61, 67, 76, 78, 79, 81, 83, 84, 91
 dummy, 50, 57, 59, 61, 65, 67, 76–77, 78, 82, 83, 92
 independent, 42, 51, 83, 88, 92
 lagged wage, 80
 nuisance, 54, 62
 seasonal and compositional, 59–62, 72, 76–77, 78, 92, 93
 specification of, 43–46
 time-trend, 65, 66, 92
 trend-dominated, 50
Violence, 6
Von Neumann, John, 4, 6

Wachter, Michael L., 2n
Wage adjustments, 46–50, 82, 86n, 87
Wage-bill hypothesis, 23
Wage equations, 1–2, 21, 27, 29–39, 40–50, 75–85, 86–89
Wage guideposts, 50
Wage maximization, 23, 25
Wage rates, 1, 23, 24, 30, 46, 47
 and average hourly earnings, 52–55, 70, 73
 and earnings, 80
 elasticity of, 36, 38, 50, 79, 80, 81
 equilibrium level of, 48–49
 influence of unions on, 86–88

Wage rates (continued)
   nonunion, 21, 35, 40, 42, 44, 48, 70–72, 73, 80, 81, 83, 88–89, 93
   and variable construction, 52–55
   and prices, 34, 36–38
   and productivity, 78
   and profits tax, 31, 32–36
Wage rounds, 46–47
Wage surplus, 22–23, 27
Wages, lagged, 80, 82, 86n, 87
Wagner, Harvey M., 7n
Walton, Richard E., 16n
Weiss, Leonard W., 31n
Wharton School utilization index, 65, 90, 92
Wilson, Thomas A., 2n, 46–48, 86, 88
Withdrawal from industry, 6, 23
Wyss, David, 62, 90, 92

Zeuthen, F., 15, 16, 19–20